THE ROUND BRITAIN QUIZ BOOK

THE ROUND BRITAIN QUIZ BOOK

PAUL BAJORIA

Foreword by Tom Sutcliffe

BBC
BOOKS

1 3 5 7 9 10 8 6 4 2

BBC Books, an imprint of Ebury Publishing
20 Vauxhall Bridge Road,
London SW1V 2SA

BBC Books is part of the Penguin Random House group
of companies whose addresses can be found at
global.penguinrandomhouse.com

Penguin
Random House
UK

This book is published to accompany the BBC Radio 4
broadcast *Round Britain Quiz*

First published by BBC Books in 2019

www.penguin.co.uk

Text: Paul Bajoria
Design: Clarkevanmeurs Design Ltd
Images: All © Getty (except Bash Street postage stamp © Stan Pritchard /
Alamy Stock Photo)

A CIP catalogue record for this book is available from the British Library

ISBN 9781785944642

Typeset in 8.5/11 pt Gill Sans
by Integra Software Services Pvt. Ltd, Pondicherry

Printed and bound in Great Britain by Clays Ltd, Elcograf S.p.A.

CONTENTS

FOREWORD

It's easy to forget that the pleasure of a good scratch usually depends on the quality of the original itch. Some itches are simple, shallow affairs – barely thought of and thoughtlessly flicked away. But some itches are resistant to easy friction – maddeningly persistent, multi-layered affairs that will only eventually yield to attacks from all sides. And scratching a self-inflicted itch might be one definition of the quiz show, or at least one explanation of their durable popularity; in a world of unappeasable irritations here is one that we know, with certainty, will pass. An episode of *Round Britain Quiz*, for example, should offer eight really top-class itches per episode, thoughtfully contrived to make it no simple matter to achieve relief. In some cases, for some people at some particular times, it may even turn out to be practically impossible – as fruitless an endeavour as scratching your right elbow with your right hand – and someone else will have to step in and help.

For the last 12 years that's been me, the latest in a long line of presenters whose task it has been to put *RBQ* contestants into a state of mild cerebral misery and then get them out of it again. And it's a long line of presenters because *Round Britain Quiz* is, by some distance, the longest running quiz on the air, certainly in this country and probably anywhere. Exactly how old it is depends on whether you include its immediate predecessor – *The Transatlantic Quiz*, a wartime, alliance-boosting collaboration with the Blue Network in New York, which introduced itself as an 'unrehearsed, spontaneous programme … carried on across 3,000 miles of ocean and brought to you by short wave transcription'. When the Sterling Crisis of 1947 threatened the survival of this transatlantic co-production, Norman Collins, then Controller of the Light Programme (also commissioner of another of Radio 4's most venerable programmes – *Woman's Hour*) was clearly anxious to avoid a break. 'While we have been waiting for the Treasury and the Bank of England to make up their minds about dollars,' he wrote in September of that year, 'time has been running very short and if we are to maintain continuity with the "Quiz" – and for a variety of reasons I am extremely anxious that this should be so – the first "Trans-Britain Quiz" should be on the air on Sunday, November 2nd.' After some dithering over the title – both 'Trans-Britain Quiz' and 'Cross-Country Quiz' were contenders for a while – *Round Britain Quiz* was approved, with the famously peppery Gilbert Harding as the first travelling quiz-master and Lionel Hale continuing his role as the London question setter.

The programme retained the dual studio, dual quiz-master format, with a regular London team competing each week with different regional teams from around the country. And there was a faint but distinct sense of metropolitan condescension in Collins's brief to his producers: 'the general guiding line about questions should, I think, be that all questions directed to the permanent team in London should be entirely general and that questions from the team in London to the Regional team should be general with a flavouring (say two questions among the lot) of Regional reference.' Interestingly, in the foreword to a predecessor of this book – published in 1950 – one of the regular London contestants, the equally peppery D. W. Brogan, implies that a lofty impartiality was not expected of the local quiz-master, writing of him as 'watching with jealous care over the interests of his team'. Over the years the essential nature of the quiz – tough questions couched in a cryptic manner – has remained the same as production methods changed. These days each series is recorded over a long weekend at a country house somewhere in the British Isles, the contestants gathering from all corners of the country like the cast of an Agatha Christie murder mystery, to face-off across a hotel conference room during the day and compare their wounds in a hotel dining room in the evening.

It was, from the start, thought of as a contest of 'wit and knowledge', not just knowledge alone. Brogan approvingly cites a story about the nineteenth-century scientist Lord Kelvin who, stumped for a rather simple astronomical fact during a lecture to undergraduates, sent a student to his office to look it up for him, specifying exactly on which shelf, how many books in from the left, and on what page of the book the required fact would be found. 'It is no part of a gentleman's education to know details,' Kelvin said grandly to the class, when the student eventually returned with the answer, 'He should know where they are to be found.' Something of that patrician disdain for mere 'details' has – let's face it – always been part of the *Round Britain Quiz* recipe, though judging from some of the questions in the 1950 anthology it didn't always make it through to the question setters. Today's teams would be bemused, and surely grateful, to be presented with questions as flatly straightforward as these: 'Can you give three quotations from song, poetry or prose about kissing?' or 'Can you name 3 of the United States of America whose names begin with the letter C?' Even when the question is a little more cryptic – 'What bullseye was often hit in *Oliver Twist?*' for example – they are distinctly one note by current standards.

These days, I'm glad to say, none of those would pass muster. The perfect *Round Britain Quiz* question now consists of three or four red herrings swimming in close formation, the true direction of which will only become clear when the conundrum is solved. What's more, the solution will ideally bring that distinct glow that comes from seeing apparently disparate and unrelatable facts slot neatly into an explanation that was invisible and now seems inevitable. It's oddly reminiscent of what Freud writes in *The Interpretation of Dreams*, about the lifelong quiz of our own subconscious:

Suppose I have a picture-puzzle, a rebus, in front of me. It depicts a house with a boat on its roof, a single letter of the alphabet, the figure of a running man whose head has been conjured away, and so on. Now I might be misled into raising objections and declaring that the picture as a whole and its component parts are nonsensical. A boat has no business to be on the roof of a house, and a headless man cannot run. Moreover, the man is bigger than the house; and if the whole picture is intended to represent a landscape, letters of the alphabet are out of place in it since such objects do not occur in nature. But obviously we can only form a proper judgment of the rebus if we put aside criticisms such as these of the whole composition and its parts and if, instead, we try to replace each separate element in some way or other. The words which are put together in this way are no longer nonsensical but may form a poetical phrase of the greatest beauty and significance.

The very best *Round Britain Quiz* questions, thanks to setters both professional and amateur, will similarly begin in baffling surrealism and end in a kind of poetry.

Trusting the subconscious will help, quite frequently – since the mind often appears to have its own equivalent of Kelvin's biddable undergraduate – an inner demon that vanishes from the room and returns quite unexpectedly with the necessary fact. At that point, during recordings, I'll usually hear a noise. The muttering that indicates frustration will give way to a little sigh of recognition. The 'ah' of a breakthrough is quite distinctive and, judging from archive recordings, unchanged over the decades. Where accents and attitudes have often changed significantly, sometimes comically so, that impulsive human response to the dawning of the light seems to be timeless. There is, sadly, no guarantee that it won't precede an answer of dazzlingly ingenious wrongness. Contestants on *Round Britain Quiz* don't just bark up the wrong tree sometimes; they climb it, construct a spacious and sturdy treehouse and then begin to fill it with bits of second-hand furniture. And they can get distinctly crestfallen when you insist that they climb down again and look in another part of the wood. That is part of the pleasure for listeners, of course – a pleasure that will be even more refined if they have themselves managed to work out the correct answer. But even listeners still in the dark can enjoy the sound of cleverness confounding itself. As Marcus Berkmann, a regular contestant for the South of England, pointed out in a piece celebrating the seventieth anniversary of the programme, 'You have to relax because the questions are so hard that the worst you can do is very badly indeed. But listeners seem to quite like that, as long as you are entertaining as you fail.' It is one of the distinctive marks of a good question that it will always have at least one loose thread that the teams can begin to unpick, so that we can enjoy them diligently following it to entirely the wrong conclusion.

For the quizmaster the challenges are a little different. I know the answers but I have no idea which route the teams are going to take on the way to them. And more often than not my guidance is sought when the contestant has travelled a long way down the backroads of their own knowledge. 'Ah ... Yes! ... Now ... could we be talking about the seventh session of the Second Council of Nicea here?' someone will ask, a look of quiet satisfaction already beginning to form on their face. Which is a question you can only satisfactorily answer if you know what was actually discussed at the seventh session of the Second Council of Nicea. If you don't, a slightly feeble 'possibly' is the only workable response, usually coupled, in my case, with a panicked look towards *Round Britain Quiz*'s long-running producer Paul Bajoria, a man whose general knowledge is measureless and who also, helpfully, has very eloquent eyebrows. His breadth of knowledge is not always helpful; a few seasons ago Paul included a question which depended on knowing what the Maunder Minimum is (it's a notable late seventeenth-century dearth of sunspots, if you're curious). My protest, that none of the six or seven people on Earth who might know this fact were actually taking part in *Round Britain Quiz* that year, was dismissed by Paul as too pessimistic. When the question came up I think we gave the team 1 point out of sheer remorse and, ever since, 'Maunder Minimum' has become a shorthand for the completely unplayable lie, the *Round Britain Quiz* equivalent of finding your golf ball plugged inside a cast-iron drainpipe.

Which brings us to the scoring – the one enigma on *Round Britain Quiz* which will probably never be satisfactorily resolved. The rough rule of thumb here is that you start with 6 points and lose 1 for every substantial nudge you have to be given. But we're in the realm of art here not science, and listeners at home – baffled by what occasionally appears to be a disjunction between performance and reward – aren't always aware that a lot of stumbling and coaxing may have been tidied out of the final edit. (There *is* an appeal to listening to an intellect in trouble, but there's only so much silence Radio 4 is happy to broadcast.) In any case, an inaudible conclave has usually taken place before the more problematic awards, a look of appeal from me being followed by a show of fingers from the show's crucial, but unheard contributors: Lizzie Foster, the programme's assistant producer; Phil Booth, the sound engineer; and Paul himself. Paul is forgivingly generous, Lizzie is sternly demanding, and between those two poles we collectively get something that approximates justice. There is no appeals procedure, which doesn't, of course, stop teams from trying.

If the question is a good one, though, even those sent away with only 1 point have the consolation of resolution. They racked their brains over something that didn't make sense, and now it does, a consummation that the world at large doesn't offer nearly often enough. Relish that feeling if you achieve it by thought alone as you tackle the questions in this book. Judge yourself kindly if you don't – every piece of knowledge is a Maunder Minimum if you've never encountered it before. But either way, enjoy the itch.

ROUND 1

We start with ten questions that we hope won't prove too tricky, and which should help you get used to the way typical *Round Britain Quiz* questions work.

Q1

Why might Atticus's daughter, Jay Silverheels's horse and Haydn Dimmock be drawn to the highest point in the Peak District?

CLUES

- Atticus's daughter is a fictional character but Jay Silverheels and Haydn Dimmock were real people.
- The highest point in the Peak District was the scene of a famous trespassing incident.

Q2

If Edinburgh's a bit hard of hearing and Inverness gives you the needle, why is Coventry proud of its achievements? And what's saucy about Hemel Hempstead?

CLUES

- You need to address yourself particularly carefully to the wording of this question.
- By the same logic, Maidstone is self-centred and Bristol talks complete rubbish.

A1

The common link is the word Scout.

Atticus's daughter, the child narrator of the Harper Lee novel *To Kill a Mockingbird*, is Jean Louise Finch, known throughout as **Scout**. Mary Badham played her in the 1962 movie (which starred Gregory Peck as Atticus).

Jay Silverheels played Tonto in the long-running US television series *The Lone Ranger*; Tonto's horse was called **Scout** (the Lone Ranger's was Silver).

Haydn Dimmock, children's writer and editor, edited the boys' magazine ***The Scout*** between 1915 and 1954. He invented the famous Boy Scout tradition of 'Bob-a-Job Week', and promulgated the idea in the magazine.

They may all be drawn to the highest point in the Peak District, which is the summit of Kinder **Scout** (636 m). Kinder Scout was the scene of a mass trespass in April 1932, by people protesting at being excluded from private land in areas of natural beauty. It's often seen as having given important momentum to the National Park movement.

A2

This is about UK postcodes.

Edinburgh is **EH**, which makes it a bit deaf (eh?).

Inverness is **IV** (intra-venous).

Coventry is proud of its **CV.**

Hemel Hempstead's postcode is **HP** (as in HP sauce).

Q3

Why would Steve Bell and Lindsay Anderson feel at home on an island fortress off Marseille?

CLUES

- The island fortress is the scene of one of the most daring escapes in fiction.
- Rudyard Kipling and Telly Savalas might feel at home there too.

Q4

Which Scottish church has been linked, at various times, with a self-mutilating painter, a young man with a horn and a crucified rebel slave?

CLUES

- The church is generic, rather than specific.
- The painter, the young man and the slave were all real people, immortalized in a particular way.

A3

The answer is: because the island fortress is called If.

The island of **If**, off the French Mediterranean coast near Marseille, has a castle dating from the 1520s which was featured as the place of imprisonment of the hero Edmond Dantès in the Alexandre Dumas novel *The Count of Monte Cristo* (1844–5). In one of literature's all-time classic pieces of derring-do, Dantès makes his escape from the *château d'If* after 14 years' incarceration, by taking the place of a dead fellow prisoner, being sewn into a burial shroud and tipped over the wall into the sea.

The British director Lindsay Anderson's ***If …*** (1968) was the first film in an increasingly surreal anti-establishment trilogy, starring Malcolm McDowell as Mick Travis. In it, he and a group of classmates enact their fantasy of causing mayhem at their hidebound public school by taking up positions on the battlements and machine-gunning half of the staff and pupils to death. The other two films in the sequence are *O Lucky Man!* (1973) and *Britannia Hospital* (1982).

Since 1981 Steve Bell (b.1951) has drawn and written the savagely satirical *Guardian* strip cartoon ***If …***

A4

The Scottish church is a kirk – because the question refers to three people portrayed on screen by Kirk Douglas.

Kirk Douglas's performance as **Vincent van Gogh** (1853–90) in *Lust for Life* (dir. Vincente Minelli, 1956) is regarded as one of the finest of his career; he went so far as to take extensive painting lessons to prepare for the role. Van Gogh cut his own ear off on 23 December 1888 in an incident the exact circumstances of which are still disputed.

Bix Beiderbecke (1903–31), the pioneering white cornet player who became one of the jazz lifestyle's earliest and most notorious casualties, inspired Dorothy Baker's novel *Young Man with a Horn*, which was filmed in 1950 by Michael Curtiz. In the film, Kirk Douglas's supposed horn playing was dubbed by Harry James.

The real historical **Spartacus**, the slave born in Thrace who was trained at gladiatorial school in order to make him marketable to coliseum owners as an (expendable) attraction in the amphitheatre, led a rebellion of some 70,000 slaves against the Roman Empire in c.73 BC. He was actually hacked to death in battle rather than crucified, as he is in the Stanley Kubrick movie of 1960. Kirk Douglas starred alongside Laurence Olivier, Peter Ustinov, Tony Curtis and Charles Laughton; Jean Simmons played his wife Varinia.

Q5

Can you place in order Dorothy's aunt, Arthur's foster brother, Dakota's sister and *Garrulus glandarius*?

CLUES

- By Dorothy in this case we mean the character in *The Wizard of Oz*.
- These are single-syllable answers.

Q6

If 509 is a German painter and 601 is a senior police officer, can you explain why 1009 is a cowboy and 1200 an entire cricket team?

CLUES

- The painter and the cowboy have surnames that rhyme.
- 501 would be a slightly *less* senior police officer.

A5

The four elements in the question give us Em, Kay, Elle and Jay – so the correct (alphabetical) order is clearly Jay, Kay, Elle and Em.

Dorothy's aunt in *The Wizard of Oz* (1939) is Aunt **Em**. After Dorothy runs away from home, early in the film, she is shown a crystal ball by the fortune teller Professor Marvel, in which Aunt Em is apparently dying of a broken heart, prompting her to rush home. In the movie Aunt Em was played by Clara Blandick.

Dakota's sister is a reference to **Elle** Fanning (b.1998), the actor sister of Dakota Fanning, whose most notable roles have included 11-year-old Cleo in *Somewhere* and Alicia in *The Beguiled*, both directed by Sofia Coppola.

Sir **Kay**, in many re-tellings of the legend of King Arthur including T. H. White's classic *The Once and Future King* and the animated Disney movie *The Sword in the Stone*, is the foster brother of Arthur. He becomes a Knight of the Round Table and Arthur's steward.

Garrulus glandarius is the bird known as the **jay**, widespread across Europe and Asia. (The bird known as a jaybird or blue jay in North America is an entirely different species.)

A6

This is an old-fashioned *RBQ* question involving Roman numerals which spell out names or abbreviations in English.

The painter is Otto **DIX** (Roman numerals for 509), twentieth-century German realist artist bitterly opposed to, and suppressed by, Nazism.

By the same logic, 601 in Roman numerals gives us **DCI** – a senior police rank.

So 1009 is **MIX**, giving us the screen cowboy Tom Mix (Thomas Hezekiah Mix, 1880–1940), Hollywood's first superstar of Westerns.

And 1200 is the **MCC** (Marylebone Cricket Club).

Q7

Where and why does a Welsh island turn up in Cambridgeshire, a Yorkshire city in Kent and an Essex town (with acute political instincts) near Reading?

CLUES

- These could all confuse an unwary visitor to Britain.
- There's a stately quality to this question.

Q8

If Abba recorded a minus two, Fleetwood Mac a minus three and Simon & Garfunkel a minus four, what might we be talking about?

CLUES

- This is nothing to do with chart positions, millions of albums sold or awards won.
- If you aren't confident of the answer you might need to wing it.

A7

In the names of three stately homes or castles, those names being most readily associated with somewhere else entirely.

Anglesey Abbey, a few miles northeast of Cambridge, a mostly sixteenth-century former priory restored by the 1st Baron Fairhaven in the 1930s, was acquired by the National Trust in 1966.

Leeds Castle in Kent is one of the most picturesque of all English castles, famous for its lake setting on two islands, the halves of the castle joined by an arched bridge. The smaller half, known as the Gloriette, was mostly built by Henry VIII.

Basildon Park is an eighteenth-century house and estate in Berkshire, near Pangbourne on the Thames. The town of Basildon is often seen as a key predictor of the outcome of a general election: its result is declared early and its swing often closely mirrors that in the country as a whole.

A8

This is not about album sales or number ones, but about golf.

Two under par in golf is an **eagle**, and Abba's song 'Eagle' was a highlight of *Abba: The Album* released in 1978.

Three under is an **albatross**, a title with which Fleetwood Mac (in their original all-British 1960s incarnation) had an instrumental no. 1 hit.

And four under, very rare indeed, is a **condor** – as in the song on Simon & Garfunkel's *Bridge Over Troubled Water* album, 'El Condor Pasa'.

Q9

If a gathering includes 12 who are religious, 13 who are guiltless, 13 who are courageous and 8 who are city-dwellers, why would only one make an impression – and who are they all?

CLUES

- In fact all of them might be said to be religious, but 12 proclaim it in a particularly obvious way.
- As so often with the people in *Round Britain Quiz* questions, they could never meet in real life. Thinking of them as a succession, rather than a gathering, may help.

Q10

Why do the following seem all confused: the one whom Roy's drowning girl refuses to call for help; an Elizabethan woman of easy virtue; and a suit of armour for a horse?

CLUES

- 'Roy's drowning girl' is a reference to a famous painting.
- A knowledge of historical vocabulary is very useful for this question.

A9

They are Popes, and the references are to the number of times these Papal names have been used throughout history.

There have been 12 Popes called **Pius**; 13 called **Innocent**; 13 called **Leo** (and thus surely courageous); and 8 called **Urban**.

And the one who would leave an impression is Pope **Mark** – there has only ever been one of these, in AD 336.

A10

They seem confused because they're mixed up, in the sense that they're anagrams of one another.

Roy Lichtenstein's painting *The Drowning Girl* (1963) depicts (in his trademark ultra-magnified comic-book style) a girl losing consciousness as she's pulled under the waves, and a thought-balloon coming from her head which reads, 'I don't care! I'd rather sink than call **Brad** for help.' In another similar canvas from the same year, a blonde girl sits wringing her hands, looking out of the picture with the caption, 'I know how you must feel, Brad'. It's a name that conveys an instant image of a stereotypical all-American male.

A **drab** is a Shakespearean word for a low-life prostitute. In one of the witches' scenes in *Macbeth*, where they list the recipe for their infernal stew, one of the ingredients is 'Finger of birth-strangl'd babe / Ditch-deliver'd by a drab'. In contemporary parlance to 'go drabbing' was to go out visiting brothels.

Medieval armour-plating for a horse was called a **bard** – usually consisting of large linked metal plates to protect the horse's flanks and exposed breast during battle or jousting. As you'd imagine, they were often very heavy and likely to impair the horse's movement.

ROUND 2

Q1

What do you have to *move* to turn a measurement of the hardness of a substance into the units in which electrical resistance is expressed? And what would you then have to move to make it all stationery?

CLUES

- In *Round Britain Quiz*, what looks like a spelling mistake often turns out to be deliberate.
- The measurement of hardness and the units of resistance are both named after German scientists.

Q2

What title might Conan Doyle have given to a group portrait featuring a Southern belle, the enemy of the Mysterons and a loyal companion of Robin?

CLUES

- If you're thinking Batman, you shouldn't be.
- If, on the other hand, you're thinking Gerry Anderson's puppets, that's helpful.

A1

You have to move the initial letter in each case.

The **Mohs** scale of mineral hardness was devised in 1812 by the German mineralogist Friedrich Mohs (1773–1839). Based on tests to find 'what scratches what', it grades minerals in a randomly ascending scale from talc (1) through gypsum (2), calcite (3), fluorite (4) and so on up to diamond (10). Other substances can be (and have been) assigned Mohs values, so that a fingernail is at 2.5 on the Mohs scale, a copper penny 3 and a pane of reinforced glass about 7.

So, move the M, and you have **Ohms**, the SI units of measurement of electrical resistance, devised by and named after physicist Georg Ohm (1789–1854). Defined as the proportionality of current and voltage in any resistor (R = V/I), the ohm is represented by the Greek letter omega Ω.

And then by moving the O, you get **HMSO**, or Her Majesty's Stationery Office, respected purveyor of pre-gummed Manila envelopes and other such indispensable materials to the civil service and all government institutions. So 'stationery' is not a spelling error at all, but very deliberate.

A2

The answer would be *A Study in Scarlet* – the title Arthur Conan Doyle actually gave to the first full-length Sherlock Holmes novel (published 1888) – because these people are all called Scarlet (or Scarlett).

Scarlett O'Hara, the wilful heroine of Margaret Mitchell's novel *Gone With the Wind* and of the 1939 film in which she was played by Vivien Leigh.

Captain **Scarlet**, leader of the futuristic fighter-pilot team 'Spectrum' in the Gerry Anderson puppet TV series that bore his name. First shown in September 1967, it was the follow-up to the massively successful *Thunderbirds*, and gave the world the catchphrase: 'This is the voice of the Mysterons!' (The voice was all there was – the alien Mysterons remained resolutely and dangerously invisible throughout the series save for mysterious green circles of light.)

If you've got this far you'll probably realize by now that the 'companion of Robin' is not Batman, but Will **Scarlet**, one of the floating population of 'merrie men' present in even the earliest versions of the Robin Hood legend. Sometimes his name is rendered as 'Scarlock', suggesting the colour of his clothing may be a later fabrication based on a misreading of his name.

Q3

What simple subtraction would cause: a catastrophic breakage to become a milliner; a duel to become a verbal game; lethal violence to result in hilarity?

CLUES

- 'Simple subtraction' is a neat alliterative phrase, not used accidentally.
- The subtraction is the same each time.

Q4

William Somerset's search for a serial killer; Guido Anselmi's search for inspiration; and George Webber's search for a beautiful woman: why are they numerically equidistant?

CLUES

- All of these names are fictional characters.
- We've given them to you in ascending order.

A3

In each case the letter S has to be removed from the beginning of the first word, to give you the second.

shatter minus s = **hatter**

swordplay minus s = **wordplay**

slaughter minus s = **laughter**

A4

These are well-known films whose titles consist solely of numbers: *Seven* (or *Se7en*), *8½* and *10*. Just to make it slightly more challenging, they're identified by the names of their leading characters, rather than the actors who played them.

Morgan Freeman plays the detective William Somerset in ***Se7en***, David Fincher's 1995 film about two detectives' desperate hunt for a serial killer who justifies his crimes as absolution for the world's ignorance of the Seven Deadly Sins. Each killing imitates one of those Sins: an obese man is made to force-feed himself to death in a version of Gluttony, while, on the other hand, a drug dealer is strapped to a bed and slowly starved to death to represent Sloth.

The part of Guido Anselmi is played by Marcello Mastroianni in the 1963 film *Otto e Mezzo* (or ***8½***, as it's usually rendered in English). Anselmi, a film director not unlike Federico Fellini, attempts to dream his way out of the director's block he is experiencing while working on his new film, a curious mix of science fiction and autobiography. The title came from the number of films Fellini reckoned he had made to that date (seven features and three shorts).

Dudley Moore played George Webber in Blake Edwards's ***10***, a hit film of 1979. It's the story of a songwriter's pursuit of a mysterious woman who scores a perfect 10 in his personal ranking system. The 'perfect' woman in question was played by Bo Derek.

Q5

If I swim back to a Nevada city, where I play a board game and I learn where to go dancing, what language do I speak?

CLUES

- This question wouldn't work if we said 'you' rather than 'I'.
- The Nevada city is not the state capital, and it's not the state's largest city, but it is famous.

Q6

These three all had a no. 1 hit in 1958. What was it called?

CLUES

- The hit you're looking for is a rock 'n' roll classic, but it's not by Elvis.
- The rugby league player is the all-time record English try scorer.

A5

Latin.

The Latin verb for 'I swim back' is **Reno** – giving us the gambling city in Nevada; the Latin for 'I play' is **Ludo** – a board game; and the Latin for 'I learn' is **Disco**.

A6

If you put the three names together you'll realize their hit was called 'Great Balls of Fire', because they are Peter the Great, Ed Balls and Martin Offiah.

The picture is of the Bronze Horseman statue in Senate Square in St Petersburg, depicting Peter the **Great**, completed in 1782. It's the work of the French sculptor Étienne Maurice Falconet, and legend has it that, as long as the statue stands, the city of St Petersburg can never fall.

Before becoming arguably even more famous as a contestant on *Strictly Come Dancing* in 2016, Ed **Balls** (b.1967) was the MP for the Yorkshire constituency of Morley and Outwood (and before that for Normanton), and served in the cabinets of Tony Blair and Gordon Brown from 2006 to 2010.

Martin **Offiah** was the extremely quick rugby league wing – inevitably nicknamed 'Chariots'. Perhaps his most impressive achievement was beating the Widnes club record for most tries in a season in his debut year of 1987–8.

'Great Balls of Fire' by the flamboyant Jerry Lee Lewis (b.1935) was recorded and released in 1957 and reached the top of the British charts in January 1958. It was the biggest of a short string of hits on Sun Records which also included 'Whole Lotta Shakin' Goin' On' and 'Breathless'. His popularity suffered a blow from which it never recovered when he married Myra Brown, his 13-year-old first cousin once removed, in 1958.

Q7

If you subtract an Agatha Christie sleuth and a musical based on H. G. Wells from a Lancashire folk group, how much are you left with?

CLUES

- All three of these things represent pretty good value.
- It may all make more sense if your memory extends back before 15 February 1971.

Q8

Can you explain why a family of medieval correspondents in Norfolk, a professor of Chemistry at the Sorbonne and a writer who declined the Nobel Prize for Literature are all rooted in history?

CLUES

- We might have said they all originate from 'another country'.
- Millions are alive today thanks to the work of this particular professor of Chemistry, and his name is used for a very common process.

A7

Nothing.

Even those too young to remember pre-decimal currency stand a chance of working this out.

The sleuth is **Tuppence**, of the husband-and-wife crime-solving partnership Tommy and Tuppence Beresford who appear in numerous adventures by Agatha Christie.

The musical, a vehicle for Tommy Steele and based on H. G. Wells's novel *Kipps*, is ***Half a Sixpence***.

And the Lancashire folk group, regularly on British TV after winning the talent show *New Faces* in 1973, was **Fivepenny Piece**. (The point of their name is that there was no such coin as a fivepenny piece – suggesting they were out-of-the-ordinary and memorable.)

A (notional) fivepenny piece, minus tuppence, minus half a sixpence (which is threepence), leaves you with nothing at all.

A8

They all begin with PAST.

They are: the **PASTon** family of Norfolk, whose letters describe domestic life in rural England from 1422 to 1509. The Paston letters were sold to Sir John Fenn, a Norfolk antiquary, and first published in 1787 – with further discoveries being made and published over the next century or so.

Louis **PASTeur** (1822–95), one of the most important figures in the history of modern science, invented the vaccine against rabies. The heating of foodstuffs to destroy harmful bacteria, known as pasteurization, is based on his discoveries. He became professor at the Sorbonne in 1867 and the Institut Pasteur was founded in 1888.

Boris **PASTernak** (1890–60), poet and translator of Shakespeare, Verlaine and Goethe. He was awarded the Nobel Prize for Literature in 1958 for his first novel *Dr Zhivago*, which was banned in the Soviet Union for being anti-Revolutionary. He was expelled from the Soviet Writers' Union and was forced to refuse his Nobel Prize, though it was finally accepted on his behalf by his surviving family many years after his death.

Q9

A play about the RAF, a film about a public school and a notoriously indiscreet political diarist would all be bad for you in excessive quantities. Can you explain why?

CLUES

- The political diarist was a Conservative MP but is more famous now as a diarist than as a politician.
- Together they would provide you with a fairly monotonous diet.

Q10

An Old Etonian vagrant favoured one in East Anglia; the unfortunate Mr Westover chose an Irish one before his obsession with a fugitive; while Mr Scherer selected one in his native USA. What is this all about?

CLUES

- Westover and Scherer were the real names of people who became famous under different names.
- So did the Old Etonian, but if we gave you his real name you would know him straightaway.

A9

They provide an unremitting diet of chips.

Chips with Everything, by Arnold Wesker (1962), is a study of class divisions in the RAF during National Service. In the play, conscript Pip Thompson is mocked for his accent and attitudes by his working-class companions Chas, Ginger and Smiler, to whom he retorts, 'You breed babies and you eat chips with everything.'

Goodbye Mr Chips, the 1939 film of a 1934 novel by James Hilton, starred Robert Donat in his defining role as a kindly public schoolmaster. 'Mr Chips' is often used as a shorthand phrase for the kind of schoolteacher who no longer exists – and perhaps never did.

'Chips' Channon – Sir Henry Channon, the backbench MP whose notoriously indiscreet diaries covering the period 1918–53 were first published in 1967. His acute observations of prominent political and social figures were shockingly candid for the time. At one point he wrote, 'What is more dull than a discreet diary? One might as well have a discreet soul.'

A10

These are three famous people who took the names of rivers as pseudonyms.

George **Orwell** (Eric Arthur Blair, 1903–50), the Old Etonian who spent some time as a vagrant (his book *Down and Out in Paris and London*, 1933, dealt with the years before he had regular writing work) took his name from the Orwell, which flows through Ipswich.

Del **Shannon**, American pop singer of the 1960s, was born Charles Westover in 1934. His biggest hit was 'Runaway'. He took his own life in 1990. The Shannon is the longest river in Ireland.

The actor Rock **Hudson** (1925–85) was born Roy Scherer Jr, later Roy Fitzgerald, later still Rock Hudson. The Hudson flows 300 miles from the Adirondack mountains, down through New York state, to New York City.

ROUND 3

Q1

The painted one, the little girl and the mother of Jesus: where did they go?

CLUES

- They're associated with a rather significant 'discovery'.
- Translating the phrases might help you.

Q2

What would Fred Hoyle think of a writer of pulp Westerns, a Restoration Archbishop of Canterbury, a penal reformer and British India?

CLUES

- In real life Fred Hoyle would have had to have lived for a few more years to see this connection.
- The four clues should give you four first names.

A1

To America with Columbus: they are the three ships of his 1492 expedition.

Pinta means 'the painted one' or 'the spotted one'. The so-called 'first sighting of the New World' was by Rodrigo de Triana from the *Pinta* on 12 October 1492.

Niña means 'little girl' (the female equivalent of '*el Niño*' or 'little boy', as in the ocean current). The *Niña* replica, built in 1992, sails the world as a travelling Columbus museum and is the most famous of the three replica ships that currently exist.

The third and largest of the three ships was the ***Santa María***, whose full name was in fact *Santa María de la Inmaculada Concepción* – unambiguously named for the mother of Christ.

A2

Astronomer Sir Fred Hoyle, FRS (1915–2001) is known for his vehement opposition to the model of the creation of the universe known as the 'Big Bang' theory. You can probably see where this is going.

Hoyle's contention was that the 'Big Bang' theory of the origin of the universe was pseudo-science, and he favoured the model known as the Steady State theory. The very phrase 'The Big Bang' was coined by Hoyle in a BBC radio interview in which he intended it as a scornful putdown.

Elmore **Leonard** (1925–2013) made his name writing pulp Westerns in the 1950s, but later turned to crime novels and screenplays. His best known stories include *Mr Majestyk, The Big Bounce, Get Shorty* and *Rum Punch*, which was adapted by Quentin Tarantino as *Jackie Brown*.

The Archbishop of Canterbury in 1663–77 was Gilbert **Sheldon**, who would be utterly obscure if he hadn't also been Chancellor of Oxford University and commissioned the Sheldonian Theatre, designed by Sir Christopher Wren and completed in 1669.

The Howard League for Penal Reform is named after John **Howard** FRS (1726–90), philanthropist and prison reformer. It was founded long after his death, in the 1860s, but took up the cause of many of the same basic improvements in prison conditions for which he had argued.

The period of British rule in India, from the early seventeenth century until after the Second World War – especially in its Victorian and Edwardian pomp – is popularly known as the **Raj**.

Leonard (Hofstadter), Sheldon (Cooper), Howard (Wolowitz) and Raj (Koothrappali) are the four nerdy student heroes of the TV sitcom *The Big Bang Theory* (2007–19).

Q3

Where would you be most likely to find a durable Welsh-language soap opera, a plant with bell-shaped flowers and a highwayman hanged in 1670?

CLUES

- The highwayman is not Dick Turpin: he is not, in fact, English, though he did pursue his activities in England.
- You're looking for phrases in more than one language.

Q4

By adding nothing, how do you turn a pulse into a comic, some clothing into Anna Christie, and a trademark into Terry Malloy?

CLUES

- By *Round Britain Quiz* standards this is a very straightforward (and typical) crossword-style question.
- Anna Christie and Terry Malloy are characters in films.

A3

In the valley.

Pobol y **Cwm** (pronounced roughly 'pobble-a-coom'), the Welsh language soap opera, is the longest continuously running soap made by the BBC, having begun in 1974 and thus pre-dating *EastEnders* by 11 years. Since 1982 it has been broadcast on S4C and is regularly that channel's highest-rated show. Its title means 'People of the Valley'.

Lily of the **Valley**, *Convolaria majalis*, is a poisonous flowering plant found in woodland, also widely cultivated in gardens, with delicate white, sweet-smelling, bell-like flowers.

Claude Du **Val** (1643–70), a Frenchman born in Normandy to a noble family who had fallen on hard times, was one of the most flamboyant and notorious highwaymen in English history. Robbing coaches travelling in and out of London, especially in the Highgate area, he was noted for his gentlemanly dress and behaviour, and, reputedly, he never used violence against his victims. A famous legend has him agreeing to let a gentleman traveller keep his possessions in return for being granted a dance by the roadside with his wife – a tale portrayed in an 1860 canvas by William Powell Frith. He was eventually arrested in the Hole-in-the-Wall tavern in Covent Garden, and hanged at Tyburn.

A4

Add the letter o (nothing) each time.

A pulse = bean + o = ***Beano***, the British children's comic first published in July 1938.

Clothing = garb + o = **Garbo**, Greta, the silent screen star (1905–90), whose first sound picture *Anna Christie* (1930, based on the play by Eugene O'Neill) was famously billed: *Garbo Talks*!!

A trademark = brand + o = **Brando**, Marlon (1924–2004), one of the all-time great screen actors. He won Best Actor Oscars for his role as Terry Malloy in *On the Waterfront* (1954), and for *The Godfather* (1972).

Q5

Why could Martha Jane Canary, Lenin's would-be assassin and a police van all provide alternative titles to a Tchaikovsky opera?

CLUES

- Martha Jane Canary is a figure from American history, better known by another name.
- If you think you have the connection, beware of showing your hand too early.

Q6

What relationship is there between two who mutilated their own feet; three who met after the battle; and Farrow, Hershey and Wiest?

CLUES

- The two who mutilated their own feet will be familiar to you but the mutilation might not.
- The last three names are actresses, as you've probably guessed. Think of a film in which they all appeared.

A5

Tchaikovsky's opera *The Queen of Spades* (premiered in St Petersburg, 1890) was based on a short story of the same name by Alexander Pushkin. The other clues give us three nicknames used by card players for the Queen of Spades: Calamity Jane, Fanny Kaplan, and Black Maria.

Martha Jane Cannary (sometimes given as Canary) was **'Calamity Jane'**. She claimed to have been Wild Bill Hickock ('Buffalo Bill')'s lover, but documentary evidence calls this into question.

Fanny Kaplan (b.1890) was executed in 1918 after she attempted to assassinate Lenin. As a teenage revolutionary she was imprisoned in Siberia for her involvement in a bomb plot. She came to view Lenin as a traitor to the revolution, and she fired three shots at him as he left a factory in Moscow in August 1918.

The police van referred to is a **Black Maria**. There are many theories as to the origin of the name, one of which is that it came from a large and powerful black lodging-house keeper named Maria Lee, who helped constables of Boston, Massachusetts in the 1830s when they needed to escort drunks to the cells.

A6

These are all about groups of sisters.

In the Grimm Brothers' version of 'Cinderella', when the Prince is trying to find the mysterious girl who left the glass slipper behind, the **Ugly Sisters** are so anxious for their feet to fit the slipper that one of them cuts off her own toe, and the other slices off part of her heel, to enable them to squeeze their feet into it. When the Prince notices the blood, he realises neither of them can be the object of his quest. This detail, like so many of the less savoury features of the Grimms' tales, is usually omitted in modern versions.

The **Weird Sisters** or the three witches, in *Macbeth*, ask one another on their first appearance: 'When shall we three meet again/In thunder, lightning, or in rain?' to which the answer is 'When the hurly-burly's done/When the battle's lost and won'.

Mia Farrow (Hannah), Barbara Hershey (Lee) and Diane Wiest (Holly) are collectively ***Hannah and her Sisters*** in Woody Allen's 1986 romantic comedy, which many consider one of the best movies of his career.

Q7

A journalist working overseas checks into a Caribbean hostelry with a Hebrew woman, using a common pseudonym for unmarried couples, and arousing the doubts of the proprietor. To which wartime sequence does this all refer?

CLUES

- The 'wartime' referred to is the Second World War.
- You're looking for five titles.

Q8

Why could the teenaged singer of 'I Will Follow Him', a dancer who was a muse to Toulouse-Lautrec and Mike Nichols's comic partner take their place among the Calendar Girls?

CLUES

- 'I Will Follow Him' dates from the 1960s.
- If you think the reference to the Calendar Girls means they all took their clothes off, think again.

A7

It refers to five titles of films made, consecutively, by Alfred Hitchcock during the Second World War.

A Caribbean hostelry might be ***Jamaica Inn***; the Hebrew woman is ***Rebecca***; the reporter is a ***Foreign Correspondent***; they check in as ***Mr and Mrs Smith***; and they arouse the proprietor's ***Suspicion***.

A8

Because their surnames are all months of the year.

Little Peggy **March** sold a million in the US in 1963 with her song 'I Will Follow Him' when she was 15 – and is still the youngest female artist to have a solo American no. 1. She became very well known in Germany, and made two bids to represent them in the Eurovision Song Contest in the 1960s and 1970s. She also had major hits as a songwriter in the 1980s and 1990s.

Jane **Avril** (1868–1943) was a Paris nightclub dancer with whom Henri de Toulouse-Lautrec became fascinated in the 1890s. Her gaunt figure, often high-kicking in a can-can, features prominently in posters he created for the Jardin de Paris, the Moulin Rouge and other nightclubs. She died in poverty and is buried in Père Lachaise Cemetery.

Film director Mike Nichols was in an improvisational theatre group, the Compass Players, in Chicago in the 1950s, with a young actress called Elaine **May** (b.1932). After splitting from the Compass Players they started performing improv comedy routines together as Nichols and May, managed by Charles H. Joffe who would later steer Woody Allen's career; and they enjoyed sell-out Broadway shows and hugely successful comedy albums. They were at their peak around 1960–1. Like Nichols, Elaine May later moved into directing films, the best known being *The Heartbreak Kid*.

Q9

The warden of Hiram's Hospital, the founder of the National Trust and a Roman assassin according to Mozart: why do they count?

CLUES

- Hiram's Hospital is not a real place.
- It may be relevant that these people were (probably) all members of large families.

Q10

Why might it be appropriate for an unscrupulous saloon-bar owner 'out west' to slip a knockout beverage to half a Tyrannosaurus rex?

CLUES

- The saloon-bar owner appears in a film.
- 'Knockout' means what it says – it doesn't just mean 'first rate'.

A9

The people in the question have names that are also ordinal numbers: Septimus means seventh, Octavia means eighth and Sesto or Sextus means sixth. Names of this kind were often given to children born into already-large families when the parents had run out of inspiration.

Septimus Harding is the eponymous protagonist of Anthony Trollope's first novel in the Barsetshire novels sequence, *The Warden*. He is the holder of that position at Hiram's Hospital, an almshouse in Barchester, and is a mild-mannered, but much put-upon, old man, who was played in a BBC adaptation by Donald Pleasence.

Octavia Hill was the eighth daughter (and ninth child) born to James Hill, hence her name. She was not only the founder of the National Trust, but also a pioneer of social housing (much influenced by her early friendship with Ruskin), a founder of the charity that became Family Action, and one of the first women to serve on a royal commission, the Royal Commission on the Poor Laws of 1905.

Sesto – also known as **Sextus** – is one of the more interesting characters in Mozart's final Italian opera, *La Clemenza di Tito* (1789). In a plot drawn from Suetonius's *Lives of the Caesars*, Sesto, a friend of the Emperor Titus, is in thrall to Vitellia, the daughter of Titus's sworn enemy, who promises his daughter to Sesto on the condition that he assassinate Titus.

A10

The key lies in the name 'Mickey Finn'

A **Mickey Finn** is a drug-laced drink, supposedly named after a dodgy Chicago bartender. He probably inspired the name of the unscrupulous saloon-bar owner at Brushwood Gulch in Laurel & Hardy's classic 1937 film *Way Out West*, played by the great James Finlayson.

And **Mickey Finn** was the name of the British percussionist (in full, Michael Norman Finn) who, in 1969, joined Marc Bolan in the pop duo Tyrannosaurus rex, which was soon to truncate its name to T.Rex and achieve monumental success. He died in 2003.

ROUND 4

Q1

An American union agitator who gave her name to a periodical; an elderly widow with a remarkable canine companion; and Arthur Lucan's alter-ego. Why might you remember them all in March?

CLUES

- The elderly widow is well known to small children, and has been for centuries.
- You'd remember them in May in the USA.

Q2

Why do an Existentialist drama, a Jacobean theatrical Parasite and a bleak rewriting of *The Coral Island* constitute a health hazard?

CLUES

- Some translation is required in this question.
- If you're baffled, go with whatever's buzzing round in your head.

A1

Because they are all known as Mother, and Mother's Day/ Mothering Sunday is traditionally celebrated in March in the UK (it's the second Sunday in May in the US).

Mother Jones (Mary Harris Jones, 1830–1930) was an Irish-born nineteenth-century campaigner for workers' rights, and is also the name of a left-wing American news magazine.

The widow with the dog is **Old Mother Hubbard** from the nursery rhyme, first printed in 1805 and among the most popular publications of the nineteenth century. The exact origin and meaning of the rhyme are disputed.

Arthur Lucan (1887–1954) was **Old Mother Riley**, a comic washerwoman character he devised in the 1930s for a music-hall act that led to a total of 16 film appearances. The act required a great deal of racing about and grotesque bodily positions. The character had a pretty daughter Kitty, played by Lucan's wife, Dublin-born Kitty McShane (1898–1964).

A2

Because they are flies, or are about flies. Flies may carry on their feet millions of micro-organisms that in a large enough dose can cause disease.

Les Mouches (*The Flies*; a play by Jean Paul Sartre, 1943); **Mosca** (meaning a fly, the title character Volpone's parasite in Ben Jonson's play of 1605); and William Golding's ***Lord of the Flies*** (1954), which consciously transposes J. M. Ballantyne's 1858 children's adventure novel *The Coral Island* into a less innocent twentieth-century setting – its chief characters Ralph, Jack and Peterkin becoming Ralph, Jack and Piggy.

Q3

Why might the chronicler of Yoknapatawpha County find it easy to handle George Sanders and the man who urged 'For God's sake look after our people'?

CLUES

- He would probably need some protective clothing nevertheless.
- The connection with the last part of the clue may not be immediately obvious, but what was his middle name?

Q4

Theoretically, why might Euclid have appreciated:

1. the site of Wyld's Great Globe at the Great Exhibition;

2. the club whose motto is *Indocilis Privata Loqui;* and

3. a mysterious bit of the Atlantic?

CLUES

- If your mind is in good shape you'll do OK at this question.
- The Great Exhibition is the one held in London in 1851.

A3

Because he is a falconer, or Faulkner, and they are both falcons.

William **Faulkner** wrote many novels about the fictional Yoknapatawpha County, which was an amalgam of the places and people familiar to him around Oxford, Mississippi. They include *As I Lay Dying* (1930), *Light in August* (1932) and *Sanctuary* (1931).

The **Falcon** was a character, originally played by George Sanders, who featured in 16 B-pictures in the 1940s. The films characters were based on the novels of Michael Arlen. After three films Sanders bored of the role and it was handed over to his brother Tom Conway, who played the Falcon's fictional brother.

Robert **Falcon** Scott died in March 1912, two weeks before the *Titanic* sank, while on an Antarctic expedition – but his body and those of his companions were not found until the November. His last, enigmatic, journal entry, on 29 March 1912, ended: 'For God's sake look after our people.'

A4

They all relate to phrases which include geometric shapes: respectively a square, a circle and a triangle. Euclid of Alexandria wrote thirteen books in which he set out a series of key geometric theorems used by mathematicians throughout history.

To coincide with the Great Exhibition of 1851 James Wyld, MP, distinguished geographer and map-maker, exhibited a giant globe in Leicester **Square** in London which became known as Wyld's Great Globe.

The Magic **Circle** was formed in 1905 by a group of twenty-three amateur and professional magicians. On the cover of the first issue of *The Magic Circular* were the signs of the zodiac which, together with the words *Indocilis Privata Loqui*, were destined to become the club's emblem. The Latin motto means 'not apt to disclose secrets'.

The Bermuda **Triangle** is a notional area off the south-eastern Atlantic coast of the US, noted for a high incidence of unexplained losses of ships, small boats, and aircraft. One theory behind the spate of disappearances is that the Triangle is one of the two places on earth where a magnetic compass points towards true north rather than magnetic north – causing navigators to get into difficulties if the compass variation or error is not compensated for.

Q5

What quality do these all share with the title character of Beethoven's only opera?

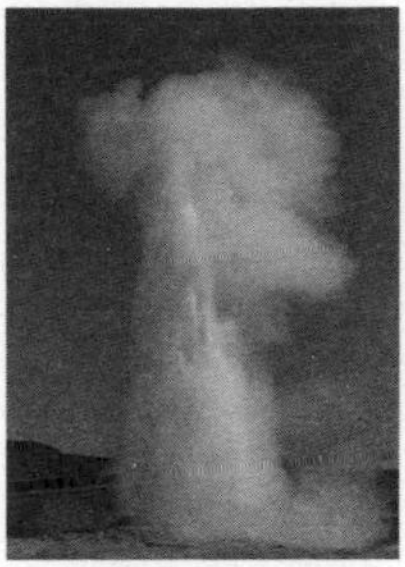

CLUES

- That's not just any old geyser: you need to know its name.
- Perhaps slightly confusingly, the opera is known by two names, as is the character.

Q6

An executioner at Tyburn in the eighteenth century might happily voyage alongside an inhabitant of the castle of Gormenghast and a hit song by Echo & the Bunnymen. Why?

CLUES

- As soon as you get one of these clues you'll sail through the rest of it.
- We're looking for a particular executioner, not just a general word for an executioner.

A5

Fidelity.

Marianne **Faithfull** (b.1946) became famous in 1964 as a singer, and a good deal more famous as Mick Jagger's girlfriend. She was a star and sex symbol for most of the 1960s but fame and hard drugs took their toll on her career and her voice. In 1979 she made something of a comeback with a critically praised, confessional album called *Broken English*. The title it was given in France, *Anglaise cassée*, points up an apposite interpretation of the title, even if it wasn't intended.

Fidel Castro (1926–2016) was Cuba's Communist revolutionary leader who came to power after the war overthrew Fulgencio Batista in 1959, and led the country for almost 50 years. He handed the reins to his brother Raúl in 2008.

The world-famous geyser in Yellowstone National Park (Wyoming) is called Old **Faithful** – named by the explorer of the American West Henry D. Washburn in 1870, and aptly so. It erupts, reliably and spectacularly, many times every day, at intervals of between three-quarters of an hour and two hours.

Fidelio is Beethoven's only opera, premiered in its original version in 1805. Beethoven originally called it *Leonore* but the Vienna theatre where it was staged insisted on changing the title to avoid confusion with other similarly titled operas popular at the time. The work went through several revisions and the title *Fidelio* is now given only to the 1814 version, earlier versions being sufficiently different to be distinguished by Beethoven's original title.

A6

The clues all point to types of sailing ship.

The eighteenth-century executioner is Jack **Ketch**, one of the most notorious operators of the Tyburn gallows, which stood on a spot near what's now Marble Arch until 1783. A ketch is a two-masted yacht.

The character in the castle of Gormenghast, from Mervyn Peake's novels *Titus Groan* (1946) and *Gormenghast* (1950), is **Barquentine**, the librarian. A barquentine is 'a three-masted vessel with the fore-mast square-rigged, the main and mizzen fore- and aft-rigged'.

The Echo & the Bunnymen hit is 'The **Cutter**' – a top-10 hit in the UK from their 1983 album *Porcupine* – a cutter being also a name for a small, fast sailing ship.

Q7

A 25-year-old beauty who struck a fatal blow for royalty, another young woman who could think of nothing to say, and a matador who couldn't stay away should suggest a common thread. Who are they?

CLUES

- Two of these are real people and one is fictional, as far as we know.
- The 25-year-old beauty is someone from French history.

Q8

At a disastrous house-party a famous drug-dealer stains a sofa, the owner of a nuclear power plant sets fire to it, and a female pop star steals some valuables. The exasperated homeowner, an explorer, imposes a financial penalty for the damage. Who is he?

CLUES

- This whole question relies on puns.
- One of these people is fictional.

A7

This one should strike a chord, or, to be precise, a CORD.

The 25-year-old aristocratic beauty who murdered the revolutionary politician Jean-Paul Marat in his bath on 13 July 1793 was Charlotte **Corday**. She was guillotined four days later.

The third daughter who could think of nothing to say – in Shakespeare's *King Lear* – was **Cordelia**.

Lear: What can you say to draw a third more opulent than your sisters?

Cord.: Nothing, my Lord.

(Act I, Scene i)

The plot of *King Lear* is taken from a supposedly 'historical' account in Ralph Holinshed's sixteenth-century *Chronicles*; but there is scant reliable evidence for any of it.

The matador who couldn't stay away was El **Cordobés** (Manuel Benítez Pérez, b.1936), the most famous Spanish bullfighter of the twentieth century, who made a comeback in 1979 after a much-publicized and much-lamented retirement from the ring in 1972.

A8

Sir Ranulph Fiennes (b.1944). He *fines* the other guests whose names all suggest other active verbs.

The drug dealer is Howard **Marks** (b.1945) who served seven years in a US high security penitentiary at Terre Haute, Indiana, for drug offences and published his autobiography *Mr Nice* in 1996 – he *marks* the sofa.

The owner of the nuclear power plant (and the only fictional character here) is Mr **Burns** (Charles Montgomery Burns) from *The Simpsons*, voiced by Harry Shearer. Obviously enough, he *burns* the sofa.

The pop star is Stevie **Nicks** (b.1948), singer with Fleetwood Mac on many of their multi-platinum albums including *Rumours*, *Tusk*, *Mirage* and *Tango in the Night*. She *nicks* the valuables.

Q9

If Act 5 Scene i of *The Tempest* reappeared in 1932, and Act 2 Scene iii of *Twelfth Night* in 1930, what happened to the third line of Sonnet 18 in 1958?

CLUES

- Shakespearean phrases have often provided inspiration for later writers.
- The third line of Sonnet 18 became even more familiar to TV viewers of a later generation.

Q10

What tasteful connection might there be between Carmen Miranda, above the neck, Josephine Baker, around the waist, and Lady Gaga, from head to toe?

CLUES

- The Lady Gaga reference concerns a widely reported incident of 2010.
- Don't make too much of a meal of this question.

A9

The clues lead to titles of twentieth-century novels lifted from Shakespeare.

So Aldous Huxley's ***Brave New World***, published in 1932, takes its three-word title from a speech of Miranda in Act 5 Scene i of *The Tempest*: 'How beauteous mankind is! O brave new world / That has such people in't'.

Somerset Maugham's ***Cakes and Ale***, published in 1930, uses part of a speech by Sir Toby Belch in Act 2 Scene iii of *Twelfth Night*: 'Dost thou think because thou art virtuous there shall be no more cakes and ale?'

The third line of Sonnet 18 is the one that goes 'Rough winds do shake the **darling buds of May**', the last five words of which were used in 1958 by H. E. Bates for the first of his five novels about the Larkin family, and subsequently for the ITV series based on them.

A10

They wore clothes made of food.

Portuguese performer Carmen Miranda (1909–55) became well known for her **fruit hats**, often very elaborate and piled very high, earning her the nickname 'the lady in the tutti-frutti hat'.

Josephine Baker notoriously wore a **skirt of bananas** in her act at the Folies Bergère in the 1920s, her striptease routine involving picking them off one at a time.

Lady Gaga appeared at the 2010 MTV Video Music Awards in a **dress (along with a little hat and big boots) made of raw beef**. It was designed by Franc Fernandez to a style by Nicola Formichetti. Lady Gaga explained the dress as a statement about the need to express publicly what one believes in, citing particularly the US Army's 'don't ask, don't tell' policy on sexual orientation.

ROUND 5

Q1

Ten in 1901; twelve in 1948; seven in 1949. What might these numbers and dates have to do with reproduction?

CLUES

- Each of these dates might be said to represent a revolution.
- If you're thinking about babies, think again.

Q2

Why might you accuse the following of sycophancy: Danger Mouse's arch-enemy, one whose life was changed by a 'Poop-poop!', and Mr Jackson?

CLUES

- You'll go a bit green when the answer is explained to you.
- Children's fiction is important in this question.

A1

This is nothing to do with childbirth, contraception or developments in fertility treatment. It's about *sound* reproduction, i.e. the format of recorded discs.

We could have worded the question as '78 in 1901, 33 and a third in 1948, and 45 in 1949'. These are the launch dates of three different disc formats that dominated the recording industry in the twentieth century – the 78 rpm disc, the LP record and the single. And the numbers relate to their typical diameter in inches.

A2

They could be accused of sycophancy because they are all toads in children's fiction (books or TV) – and are therefore, by definition, toady.

Danger Mouse's arch-enemy is **Baron Greenback**, created by Brian Trueman and voiced by Edward Kelsey, in the original children's cartoon series (ITV, 1981–92), which was revived on CBBC in 2015. He's a wheezy-voiced toad dressed in a suit and spats, his name and demeanour suggesting a stereotypical unscrupulous tycoon.

His image may owe something to Kenneth Grahame's **Mr Toad**, whose life is changed when the reckless driver of a motor car ploughs his gypsy caravan off the road in the early chapters of *The Wind in the Willows* (1908). He's left sitting in the road, stunned, repeating 'Poop-poop!' – and vows that the motor car is henceforth 'the *only* way to travel'.

Mr Jackson is the toad who invites himself for tea in Beatrix Potter's *The Tale of Mrs Tittlemouse* (1910). He comes in because he smells honey and ransacks her burrow in search of it, unmoved by her protestations that she has none. He is a more unsettling character than either of the above because (in common with most of Beatrix Potter's carefully observed characters), despite his human speech and clothes, he behaves exactly like a toad.

Q3

A naturalist, originally studying marine mammals in Cardiff but then switching to conifers in Nicosia, travels to work in Santiago but finds it too cold. He moves to hotter climes in Doha, only to suffer from mucous inflammation. He tries a spell selling lubricants in Athens, and finally settles in Seoul to spend the rest of his working life. Given his track record, where might he choose to eat Christmas dinner?

CLUES

- This is a classic *Round Britain Quiz* punning question.
- Think of where the cities are in each case, and it should start to make sense.

Q4

In what sense could a punctuation mark, a reptilian carapace, one with the power to admit or exclude and a forked harbinger of summer all be described as elusive?

CLUES

- Do any phrases spring to mind including the adjective 'elusive'?
- You're in the natural world here.

A3

The answer is Ankara. The link throughout is homophones of the countries he visits.

Studying marine mammals in Cardiff would mean he was watching **whales in Wales** ...

Switching to conifers in Nicosia (**cypress in Cyprus**) ...

He travels to work in Santiago but finds it too cold (so he'd be **chilly in Chile**).

He moves to hotter climes in Doha only to suffer from mucous inflammation (or perhaps **catarrh in Qatar**) ...

He tries selling lubricants in Athens (**grease in Greece**) ...

and later settles in Seoul to spend the rest of his working life (a **career in Korea**).

By this logic, he'd be likely to go to Ankara for a traditional Christmas dinner (thus eating **turkey in Turkey**).

A4

They are butterflies. The reference is to Bob Lind's classic hit song 'Elusive Butterfly', which flitted around in the British top 10 for several weeks in the spring of 1966 alongside Val Doonican's equally popular cover version.

Although they are elusive (and in many cases endangered) these are four of the most commonly found butterflies in Britain.

The **comma**, *Polygonia c-album*, named for the markings on its underwing which resemble the punctuation mark; the small **tortoiseshell**, *Aglais urticae* (the large tortoiseshell is sadly all but extinct in the UK); the **gatekeeper**, *Pyronia tithonus*, also known as the hedge brown; and the **swallowtail**, *Papilio machaon,* whose most notable remaining habitat is the Norfolk Broads.

Q5

Why is the link between a gallantry medal invented by George Washington and a legendary rhythm section, summed up by Alice Walker?

CLUES

- The rhythm section, rather than consisting of real musicians, is referred to in a popular song.
- The connection could be described as imperial.

Q6

What connects Sebastian Dangerfield; Fred Murray; David Lodge; political agitators; and a supporting outlaw?

CLUES

- You may have to tread your way carefully through this question.
- Geraldine Horner might also be on the list.

A5

Because the link is the colour purple.

Alice Walker wrote the novel ***The Color Purple*** (1982) which won the Pulitzer Prize and was made into a movie by Steven Spielberg in 1985.

The gallantry medal is the **Purple Heart**, first awarded by Washington for outstanding bravery in the War of American Independence and later revived on the 200th anniversary of Washington's birth in 1932. It's now awarded exclusively to those wounded or killed in the service of their country.

Elvis Presley's 'Jailhouse Rock' (1956) features the memorable line: 'The whole rhythm section was the **Purple Gang**'.

A6

Ginger.

Sebastian Dangerfield is the wayward hero of the bawdy comic novel ***The Ginger Man*** (1955), the literary debut of J. P. Donleavy (1926–2017). Donleavy's autobiography is called *The History of the Ginger Man* (1993).

The popular music-hall song (*c.*1910) **'Ginger, You're Barmy!'** is attributed to songwriter Fred Murray. The title was in turn taken by David Lodge for an autobiographical novel about National Service (published in 1962).

A small group of political agitators, often within a larger political grouping, is known as a **ginger group**.

Ginger is a friend of 'Just William' Brown, one of the 'Outlaws' in the books by Richmal Crompton (1890–1969). The other outlaws were Henry and Douglas. The first William book appeared in 1922 and she continued to publish books about him until her death.

We deliberately left out Geraldine Horner (née Halliwell) – otherwise known, of course, as Ginger Spice.

Q7

Why might Gordon express surprise at being the father of a defensive publisher, the kingdom of Croesus, *Impatiens walleriana*, a carrier of typhoid and a bowls player's target?

CLUES

- The fact that he'd be the father of five might give you a hint.
- Gordon is a real person whose name has become proverbial.

Q8

The final words of Ibsen's *Ghosts*, the final words of Mr Kurtz and the title of an Iris Murdoch novel might start to sound familiar. What are they?

CLUES

- At the risk of repeating ourselves, there is a familiar pattern in this question.
- Mr Kurtz appears in a novel, but he has a counterpart in film whose final words are exactly the same.

A7

A popular expression of surprise is still 'Gordon Bennett!' The exclamation is said to derive from the colourful exploits of James Gordon Bennett Jr, a nineteenth-century playboy and owner of the *New York Herald*.

Give or take a final 't', he shares his surname with the five sisters in Jane Austen's *Pride and Prejudice*, whose forenames are suggested by the other clues.

The 'defensive' publisher is **Jane's**, as in *Jane's Defence Weekly, Jane's Fighting Ships* and many other authoritative publications, named after Frederick Thomas Jane, nineteenth-century journalist, pulp novelist and illustrator.

Croesus was King of ancient **Lydia**, in Asia Minor, whose site on at least two major Asian trade routes contributed to its huge wealth.

Impatiens walleriana is the garden plant known as a Busy **Lizzie**.

'Typhoid **Mary**' was the nickname given to Irish-born Mary Mallon, who, as the first known healthy carrier of typhoid in the US, is thought to have infected 22 people while working as a cook in Manhattan.

Finally, a **kitty**, as well as being a cat and a pool of money, is another name for the jack, or target ball, in lawn bowls.

A8

They each consist of a short phrase repeated.

The final words of Henrik Ibsen's *Ghosts* (1881) are uttered by the dying Oswald, sitting in an armchair while the sun sets. His distressed mother is the only other person on stage. Several times in the last minutes, but resonantly as the very final line of the play, he says: **'The sun. The sun.'**

Equally disturbing are the dying words of Mr Kurtz, the mysterious ivory agent of Joseph Conrad's *Heart of Darkness* (1902). Having spent much of his life in the depths of the African jungle, driven mad, and unable to articulate the frightening reality of what he has experienced, Kurtz's final words are: **'The horror! The horror!'** Colonel Kurtz, Marlon Brando's character in *Apocalypse Now*, which takes direct inspiration from *Heart of Darkness*, speaks the very same words at the end of the film.

The novel by the late Iris Murdoch, which won the Booker Prize in 1978, is ***The Sea, The Sea***. It centres on the relationship between a theatre director and his childhood love, and draws heavily on elements of Shakespeare's *The Tempest*.

Q9

Something whose speed was measured by Rømer; an original for Sludge the Medium; and the estate of the common people. What happened in 1967 to render them obsolete?

CLUES

- Sludge the Medium is a fictional character based on a Victorian spiritualist.
- To be more precise, it happened on 30 September 1967.

Q10

These are three little pairings. One's energizing and soulful, another scientific and entrepreneurial, and a third rejuvenating and playful. What's the common letter?

CLUES

- You're looking for abbreviations that are all in quite common conversational use.
- As it happens, they are in alphabetical order.

A9

Light; Home; Third: all were BBC networks, which disappeared with the reorganization of radio in September 1967.

Ole Rømer, Danish astronomer, first measured the speed of **light** in 1676: in a vacuum it's slightly over 186,282 miles per second or roughly 300,000 km/sec.

Daniel Dunglas **Home** (1833–86), was a Scottish-born spiritualist who attracted high society to his London séances in the mid-Victorian period. He was expelled from Rome in 1864 as a sorcerer. Browning loathed the Victorian fashion for charlatan mediums, and had Home (possibly among others) strongly in mind when he satirized them in the 1864 poem 'Mr Sludge, the Medium'.

The term originating in pre-Revolutionary France, the *tiers état* or **Third** Estate was the common people, after the nobility (the First) and the Church (the Second).

A10

R & B, R & D, R & R. So the common letter is R.

They stand for **Rhythm & Blues; Research & Development; Rest & Recreation**.

ROUND 6

Q1

Why might the best-known piano work of Erik Satie make you think of Mike Leigh, William Burroughs and Jamie Oliver?

CLUES

- Satie was famous for giving his piano works obscure titles whose relevance is not immediately obvious
- Thinking of Jamie Oliver's long-standing nickname will help you

Q2

Add Hester's letter to transform: a place in Ohio into a place in Florida; an ancient Greek medic into a mineral ore of lead; and William Blake's mythical rebel hero into a killer whale.

CLUES

- This is a familiar type of *Round Britain Quiz* word-transformation puzzle.
- Hester is a fictional early settler in North America.

A1

The link is nakedness.

Satie's best known work is probably the trio of short pieces called ***Trois gymnopédies*** (1888), which take their title from an annual festival held in ancient Sparta. The Greek word *gumnos* means naked, as in derived words such as gymnasium (originally a place where people exercised naked), gymnosperm (a seed without an outer protective coating), etc.

The films of Mike Leigh (b.1943) are noted for their bleak realism and black humour, and include the acclaimed 1993 movie ***Naked***. It stars David Thewlis as a young man out of control, and is set largely in Leigh's native Manchester.

The Naked Lunch (1959) is perhaps the best known book of William S. Burroughs (1914–97), and typical of his work in combining grotesque elements of drug abuse and unconventional sex.

Jamie Oliver is known as the **Naked Chef**.

A2

Hester Prynne's letter in Nathaniel Hawthorne's *The Scarlet Letter* was the letter A (for Adulteress). By adding A to all of the first named, we arrive at the second.

A place in Ohio (**Dayton**) becomes a place in Florida (**Daytona**).

An ancient Greek medic (**Galen**, Claudius Galenus c. AD 130–201, physician to Roman emperors and a pioneering researcher into the workings of the human organs) becomes an ore of lead (**Galena**, the mineral form of lead sulphide).

Blake's mythical rebel hero in his series of complex allegorical 'prophetic books' beginning with *Visions of the Daughters of Albion*, is **Orc** – who becomes **Orca**, a killer whale, by adding an A.

Q3

An alien-hunter who was bright-eyed and bushy-tailed; an Updike hero with an infinitesimal name; and a woman who hires Marvin to get rid of Marvin. Could they safely be left in a room together?

CLUES

- 'Bright-eyed and bushy-tailed' is a reference to the alien-hunter's name, rather than being a literal description.
- The Updike hero recurs in several of his books.

Q4

What's so tragic about the creator of the Jumblies, the first book in Faulkner's Snopes trilogy, the bobby of Lochdubh and the game of Reversi?

CLUES

- The clues point to relatively modern things but the connection between them goes back four centuries.
- Reversi is known by another name in its commercial form.

A3

Probably not. These are fictional characters whose names are animals.

As **Fox** Mulder, David Duchovny hunted aliens with his partner Dana Scully (Gillian Anderson) for the FBI in *The X-Files*, the science fiction TV series created by Chris Carter, which ran from 1993 to 2002, and returned in 2016 to 2018.

Harold C. **'Rabbit'** Angstrom is the American everyman-hero in four celebrated novels by John Updike, *Rabbit Run* (1961), *Rabbit Redux* (1971), *Rabbit is Rich* (1981), *Rabbit at Rest* (1990). A novella, *Rabbit Remembered*, also appeared in 2001. An Angstrom (named after a nineteenth-century Swedish physicist) is a unit of measurement equal to a hundred millionth of a centimetre – a surname chosen by Updike to suggest Rabbit's insignificance.

Cat *Ballou* is a 1965 comedy-western film which tells the story of a woman (Jane Fonda) who hires a famous gunman (Lee Marvin) to avenge her father's murder, but finds that the man she hires isn't what she expected. Lee Marvin won an Oscar for his dual role as both the gunman and the killer he's being paid to track down.

A4

What's tragic about them is that they share the names of the eponymous protagonists of Shakespeare's four main tragedies: respectively, Lear, Hamlet, Macbeth and Othello.

The Jumblies were the invention of the artist and nonsense poet, Edward **Lear** (1812–88).

The first book in William Faulkner's 'Snopes trilogy' is *The* ***Hamlet*** (1940). The Snopes family recur in *The Town* (1957) and *The Mansion* (1959). Snopes family members also appear in earlier works *Sartoris* (1929), *As I Lay Dying* (1930) and *The Unvanquished* (1938).

In the detective stories of Scots-born journalist and novelist M. C. Beaton (pen-name of Marion Gibbons), the policeman in the Highland village of Lochdubh is Hamish **Macbeth**. In the 1990s BBC TV adaptations he was played by Robert Carlyle.

Reversi, a game of strategy for two players involving black and white discs, was invented in the 1880s, but known more recently, commercially at least, as **Othello**. *The Oxford History of Board Games* notes: 'Othello differs from Reversi only in requiring the first two pieces of each colour to be placed diagonally to one another on the four central squares, whereas Reversi merely requires the first four to be played to the centre.'

Q5

Why would an assassinated African dictator, the Prince of Wails and the children's favourite historian make Julie Andrews burst into song?

- There are quite a few assassinated African dictators; this assassination took place in 1990.
- In arriving at the connection it might help you to consult your notes.

Q6

Can you take us, in a flash, from a man who shot 26 famous seconds of film footage to a Central American revolutionary and a musical mother of invention, similarly moustachioed?

CLUES

- The revolutionary's moustache was so distinctive that the style has become known by his name.
- The musical mother, just to be deliberately confusing, is a man.

A5

Because the first three notes just happen to be: DO-RE-MI.

Samuel K. **Doe**, the leader of Liberia throughout the 1980s, proclaimed himself head of state after a coup, and gained some sort of legitimacy when he narrowly won a presidential election in 1985. After a decade in which his human rights record was hardly exemplary, he was deposed and killed by rebel forces in September 1990.

The 'Prince of Wails' was the nickname of the 1950s singer Johnny **Ray**, whose principal onstage gimmick was to shed real tears while singing hammy ballads, to the immense irritation of his critics. His hit songs included 'Cry', 'The Little White Cloud that Cried', 'Such a Night', and 'Yes Tonight Josephine'. Another of his gimmicks was that he wore a hearing-aid, though that was because of a genuine hearing disability.

The English historian Arthur **Mee** (1875–1943) wrote what is probably still the best-known children's encyclopaedia, published in 1910 as *The Children's Encyclopaedia* and in 1912 as *The Book of Knowledge*. His other works included *The King's England*, a multi-volume work devoted to the counties and landmarks of England; *The Children's Shakespeare* (1926); and an encyclopaedia entitled *I See All*, consisting entirely of pictures (1928–30).

Julie Andrews, in the part of Maria, was famously spurred into song by the phrase 'Do-Re-Mi' in the 1965 film version of Rodgers & Hammerstein's *The Sound of Music*.

A6

Zap!

The 26-second 8-mm amateur film of the shooting of John F. Kennedy in Dallas on 22 November 1963 is called the **Zapruder Film**, after the local dressmaker Abraham Zapruder who took it with his home movie camera from his vantage point on a concrete pedestal on Elm Street. In common with almost everything to do with the Kennedy assassination, its authenticity has been repeatedly questioned, one of the many points of controversy homing in on the possible alteration or falsification of the 313th of the film's 486 frames.

The revolutionary is **Emiliano Zapata** (1879–1919), icon of the Mexican revolution and ally of Pancho Villa.

The Mothers of Invention was the experimental rock group conceived and led by **Frank Zappa** (1940–93), whose trademark moustache bore a close resemblance to that of Zapata. The Mothers of Invention's recordings include *Freak Out!* (1966), *Uncle Meat* (1968) and *We're Only in It for the Money* (1969).

Q7

Why have we printed these pictures in this precise order?

CLUES

- You can always count on *Round Britain Quiz* to baffle you.
- It's not so much the name of the character in the second picture, as the name of the film from which it's taken, that will help you.

Q8

What deceitful claim to fame is shared by Frances Griffiths and Elsie Wright; Dr Robert Wilson; and Manuel Elizalde?

CLUES

- All of these deceits took place in the twentieth century.
- The incident in which Dr Robert Wilson was involved happened in Scotland.

A7

The pictures suggest the sequence, in ascending order, 999, 1000, 1001.

Dixon of Dock Green, of course, was the archetypal police TV series – to call Sgt Dixon (Jack Warner) you would have to dial **999**.

The photo depicts Geneviève Bujold in the 1969 film dramatization of the life and death of Anne Boleyn, ***Anne of the Thousand Days***. Richard Burton played Henry VIII.

The third picture is an illustration of Scheherazade, the heroine of the ***1001 Nights***. Scheherazade, the wife of Sultan Shariar, hoped to save her own life by keeping him amused with her serial stories night after night, thus distracting him from his notorious habit of having his wives executed after one night's passion.

A8

They were all the perpetrators of famous photographic hoaxes.

Two children, Frances Griffiths and Elsie Wright, claimed in 1917 to have taken **photographs of fairies** in a garden at Cottingley in Yorkshire. Despite experts' solemn testimony that there was no way the pictures could have been fakes, they confessed in their seventies that they'd created the pictures by simply cutting pictures of fairies out of a magazine.

Dr Robert Wilson was the Harley Street gynaecologist who supposedly took the most famous **photograph of the Loch Ness Monster**, showing a silhouetted head and neck rearing up out of moonlit water, and known as 'the surgeon's photograph'. It was revealed many decades later that he'd been put up to it by two friends, and that the 'monster' was a toy submarine with a plywood head. They chose to publish the photo under the doctor's name because of the respectability that gave to their story.

Manuel Elizalde was the cultural minister of the Philippines under Ferdinand Marcos, who sold **pictures of a supposed 'stone-age' tribe** called the Tasaday to the *National Geographic*. They caused a sensation – until other journalists reported finding the self-same tribe wearing T-shirts and trainers when they were later visited without warning. It turned out Elizalde was trying to divert attention from the exploitation of the jungle region by a mining company of which he was a director.

Q9

A savage creature rescued and looked after on an island; the story of a sexually voracious puppeteer; and a sort of Greek Pygmalion. Which group of Conservatives could form the next in the sequence?

CLUES

- You could say this is an everyday *Round Britain Quiz* question.
- The savage creature is not Caliban.

Q10

To take Caesar's soothsayer, with malice aforethought, to three places in New England would make a change. Can you explain why?

CLUES

- The phrase 'malice aforethought' is a legal term – but it's also the title of something.
- 'Three places in New England' is a title too.

A9

The sequence is that of the days of the week.

The savage on the island is not Caliban, as you'll have seen from the clue, but the one rescued by Robinson Crusoe and who became his companion, i.e. **Friday**.

The puppeteer is Mickey **Sabbath**, hero of *Sabbath's Theater*, the acclaimed 1996 novel by the late Philip Roth. Since Roth was Jewish, the Sabbath is Saturday.

The Greek film *Never on* ***Sunday*** (1960) is a variation on Shaw's *Pygmalion*; it's about an American scholar in Greece who meets a prostitute and sets about improving her. It starred Merlina Mercouri and was directed by Jules Dassin, and the title song won an Oscar.

So the group of Tories is the **Monday** Club, formed in 1961 by right-wingers including Julian Amery and the Marquis of Salisbury. It was so called because its members regularly lunched together on Mondays.

A10

This is about three words/names requiring a single change of letter each time: Ides – Iles – Ives.

The soothsayer in *Julius Caesar*, Act I Scene ii, famously warns Caesar to 'Beware the **ides** of March' (i.e. 15 March). In the ancient Roman calendar the 'ides' are the eighth day after the 'nones'. The ides of March, May, July and October are on the fifteenth of those months. The ides of all the other months fall on the thirteenth.

Malice Aforethought is a classic 1931 crime novel by Francis **Iles** (a pseudonym for Anthony Berkeley Cox), about a Devon doctor who poisons his wife. The title refers to an archaic legal term for the premeditation that must be demonstrated in a conviction for murder.

The American modernist composer Charles **Ives** composed 'Three Places in New England' (1904). The second section features two marching bands playing different march melodies, in different tempi, simultaneously.

ROUND 7

Q1

In what way do a hummingbird, Bruce Springsteen's disguise, a comic novel by Clive James and a diamond with 58 facets all excel?

CLUES

- This is a shining example of an opening question.
- The Clive James novel in question was his first.

Q2

An encounter that leads nowhere; a creature of limited versatility; a settlement without much excitement; Brando's only movie (in one sense); and a machine that will almost certainly rob you. What do they add up to?

CLUES

- You're looking for phrases that have a particular word in common.
- You'll soon realize that this is a singularly straightforward question.

A1

They are all brilliant.

A **brilliant** is a name given to a group of species of hummingbird, because of their especially bright colours, mostly found in Central and South America

Bruce Springsteen's song **'Brilliant Disguise'** appeared on his *Tunnel of Love* album in 1987.

Clive James's first novel was ***Brilliant Creatures*** (1983), a satire on London literary society.

A gemstone – especially a diamond – cut so that it has 58 facets is referred to as a **brilliant**.

A2

These are phrases which all involve the number one – so they add up to five.

One-night stand; one-trick pony; one-horse town; *One-Eyed Jacks* (Marlon Brando's only movie as *director*, a revenge Western of 1961); **one-armed bandit** (its nickname derives from the near-certainty that you'll be poorer after playing it).

Q3

One was celebrated for finding a trophy, another went into orbit and a third met his fate on the way back from Porlock. Who were they, and which one survived?

CLUES

- The trophy was a sporting trophy that's very famous, and valuable.
- You sometimes associate Porlock with the poet Coleridge, but not in this instance.

Q4

You'll need a long spoon if you're planning to get on a train in Aberystwyth and go to a waterfall; or to look at rocks in North Devon; or to visit a prison colony off French Guiana. Why?

CLUES

- This could prove a fiendish question.
- We could have given you a lot of other possible examples.

A3

These are three famous dogs in post-war history; Pickles survived.

Pickles, a black and white collie, found the Jules Rimet trophy a week after it was stolen in March 1966, a few months before the World Cup tournament was held in England. While out for a walk he drew his owner's attention to a package in the front seat of a car in north London, which turned out to be the trophy wrapped in newspaper. When England won the Cup, Pickles was invited to the celebration banquet. He was also named Dog of the Year and appeared on *Blue Peter.*

Laika was a stray dog from the streets of Moscow sent into orbit by the Soviet Union in November 1957 aboard Sputnik 2, to test the effects of space travel on living creatures. She died from the heat, probably within hours of the launch – although the real story wasn't made public until 45 years later, the Soviets long maintaining that she lived for six days until the oxygen ran out in the spacecraft. Nevertheless her role in the development of space flight is seen as crucial.

Rinka was Norman Scott's Great Dane, shot in October 1975 by the hired killer Andrew Newton who had allegedly been hired to shoot Scott himself, on a lonely road between Porlock and Combe Martin in Devon. The shooting was just one of a series of fiascos in the long-running feud between the Liberal Party leader Jeremy Thorpe and his former lover, and Thorpe's attempts to cover it up. The incident provided a memorable scene in the 2018 BBC TV dramatization *A Very English Scandal*, with a script by Russell T Davies.

Pickles was the only one to survive the acts that made them famous – although, rather tragically, he died of strangulation a year or so after his fame, when his choke-chain got caught in the branch of a tree.

A4

Because these are all places with the Devil in their name: and the old adage has it that 'he who sups with the Devil needs a long spoon'.

Devil's Bridge, over the dramatic Mynach Falls, is reached by a narrow-gauge railway, which takes tourists from Aberystwyth, 12 miles away.

The **Devil's Cheese Press** is a strange towering formation of eight rocks near Lynmouth in Devon.

Devil's Island was the notorious French penal colony off French Guiana to which Captain Alfred Dreyfus was sent. It was also described in Henri Charrière's bestselling novel *Papillon*.

There are many other place names and geographical features, in the UK and elsewhere, known as 'the Devil's' something.

Q5

A reclusive poet misquoted by Mrs Thatcher; a cultural revolutionary; and the greatest lover in European history, have something in common. What can we read into that?

CLUES

- The connection is not obvious just from their names: you have to know something about their biographies.
- The poet, despite her misquoting him, is known to have rather admired Mrs Thatcher.

Q6

A nineteenth-century battle could connect the wives of a great composer and the doyen of film directors; a 1950s Dreamboat singer; and languid women reclining on marble. Which battle, and why?

CLUES

- The battle in question was fought in the Crimea.
- The composer was middle-European and the director British.

A5

They were all librarians.

The poet is the famously publicity-shy **Philip Larkin** (1922–85), the librarian at the University of Hull for 30 years. When asked for a favourite line of poetry, Mrs Thatcher cited a misremembered quotation from Larkin: 'She had a mind like a knife'. Wishful thinking and surely a bit of self-flattery on the Lady's part: what Larkin wrote, in his poem 'Deceptions' in the collection *The Less Deceived*, was: 'All the unhurried day/ Your mind lay open like a drawer of knives'.

Mao Tse Tung (1893–1976), dictator and instigator of the notorious Cultural Revolution in China 1966–9, had in his early years, grotesquely, been a librarian at the University of Beijing, which is where he first read Marx and formed his enduring ideals of communism.

Casanova (Giacomo Girolamo Casanova de Seingalt, 1725–98) scandalized Europe and led what was surely one of the most colourful lives of any eighteenth-century figure. He was variously secretary to a cardinal, cleric, gambler, alchemist, violinist, imprisoned for being a magician only to make a daring escape, director of the state lotteries in Paris, knighted in the Netherlands, spy for Louis XV and lover of reputedly thousands of women. He settled down in Bohemia in 1785 as librarian to Count von Waldstein.

A6

The Battle of the Alma, fought at the Alma river in the Crimea in 1854; the others all have Alma in their name.

Alma Mahler was the wife of the composer/conductor Gustav Mahler, and became the lover of Walter Gropius, director of the Bauhaus in Dessau. (She had other lovers, including the artist Oskar Kokoschka.)

Alma Reville was one of the most prominent women in the movie industry in the 1920s to the 1940s; spotted and nurtured by Alfred Hitchcock, she became his wife in 1926 and co-wrote the screenplay for the films *The Thirty Nine Steps, The Secret Agent, The Lady Vanishes, Jamaica Inn* and *Suspicion* among others.

Alma Cogan was one of the best known British singing stars of the 1950s, who had hits with cover versions of songs originally recorded by Doris Day, Rosemary Clooney, Dinah Shore, Patti Page and Kitty Kallen. Dubbed 'the girl with the giggle in her voice', she enjoyed her biggest hit with 'Dreamboat', a UK no. 1 in 1955. She died tragically young from ovarian cancer in 1966.

'Languid women reclining on marble' is a fair way to describe the favoured subject matter of the painter **Sir Laurence (originally Lourens) Alma-Tadema** (1836–1912). His best known works are Classical scenes featuring startlingly blue Mediterranean seas, marble terraces and meticulous attention to details of clothing, which he has in common with his contemporaries the Pre-Raphaelites.

Q7

A spectator at a Shakespearean play-within-a-play and a young pretender to the throne of England could, in their way, be just as tasty as the 'thinking man's crumpet'. How so?

CLUES

- This question should suit people with a sweet tooth.
- The young pretender to the throne was aged only ten.

Q8

Starting with a man famous for what he did with a harpsichord, we progress to another man who psychoanalysed three dead giants of literature. But once we get closer to the present day we're dealing with a slimmer model altogether. Who are they, and why are they connected?

CLUES

- This question draws on more than one branch of culture.
- As so often in RBQ, it will help you if you speak more than one language.

A7

Their names are all those of cakes or tarts.

It was Frank Muir who used the phrase 'the thinking man's crumpet' of Joan **Bakewell** (Baroness Bakewell, b.1933), while she was one of the presenters on BBC2's *Late Night Line-up* (1965–72) – and, for all her journalistic and other achievements, she has not shaken it off. Bakewell tart features a shortcrust pastry shell filled with jam, sponge and ground almonds, and often iced. The supposedly more 'genuine' Bakewell pudding, still made at Bakewell in Derbyshire, is usually circular and has puff pastry.

In Shakespeare's *The Taming of the Shrew*, the drunken tinker Christopher **Sly**, having been 'vomited out of an ale-house', is discovered asleep by a lord who decides to have some fun at his expense. He persuades a passing troupe of players to perform the story of Petruchio and Katherine for Sly to watch. Sly is convinced, at the end, that he has had a vivid dream which has revealed to him the secret of how to 'tame' his wife. Sly cake is another traditional northern English tart or slice, featuring mixed dried fruit in pastry.

Lambert **Simnel** (*c.*1477–1534) was one of two impostors (along with Perkin Warbeck) who, with the backing of Yorkist conspirators, threatened the reign of Henry VII. The plot to present him as the young Earl of Warwick, a legitimate claimant to the throne, was thwarted – but the boy Simnel was pardoned, and later became a falconer in the King's household. Simnel cake is a light fruit cake a bit like a Christmas cake, covered in marzipan, often eaten at Easter. Its name is almost certainly nothing to do with Lambert Simnel, but may derive from Latin *simila*, fine wheaten flour from which the cakes were made in medieval times.

A8

They are all 'twigs'.

Jean-Philippe **Rameau** (whose name means twig) was one of the most influential composers of harpsichord music in the Baroque period.

Stefan **Zweig** (whose name also means twig) wrote *Three Masters* (1920), a collection of psychological studies, drawing heavily on the theories of Freud, of three great writers – Balzac, Dickens and Dostoevsky.

The slimmer model, naturally enough, is **Twiggy**, professional name of the Neasden-born model and actress Dame Lesley Lawson, née Hornby, one of the most instantly recognizable faces of the Swinging Sixties.

Q9

Can you rank the following according to the Beaufort scale: an adventuresome sequel by Alistair MacLean, a classic children's novel by Richard Hughes and a novella by Joseph Conrad?

CLUES

- Unsurprisingly, there is a nautical element to them all.
- It's fair to say you'll find them all at the upper end of the scale.

Q10

Why could a literary Russian awarded a Nobel Prize in the fifties, a film producer who started a great franchise in the sixties and a German politician who came to power in the eighties all have found themselves translated from WC2 to SW8 in the seventies?

CLUES

- 'Translated' is a significant word here, too.
- Few things are more tiresome for people who don't live in London than being expected to recognize London postcodes. SW8 is the postcode of Nine Elms.

A9

These are all books set on the high seas, with references to wind in their titles.

Force 10 From Navarone (1968) was the follow-up to the immensely popular naval adventure *The Guns of Navarone* (1957) by Alistair MacLean (1922–87). In the period between the two books, the original novel had been successfully filmed: and, unusually, MacLean based his sequel largely on the events and characters of the film, rather than the book.

The Welsh writer Richard Hughes (1900–76) wrote ***A High Wind in Jamaica*** (1929) about a group of children captured by pirates. Told through the children's eyes, and featuring some truly disturbing events, it has been hailed as one of the greatest literary recreations of a child's psychology. An intriguing piece of trivia is that, when the novel was filmed in 1965, one of the child actors was a young Martin Amis (then aged 15).

The Conrad novella is ***Typhoon***, published along with the short stories 'Falk', 'To-morrow' and 'Amy Foster' as *Typhoon and Other Stories* in 1903. It concerns the phlegmatic Captain MacWhirr and his encounter with a typhoon in the South China Sea.

A *typhoon* measures 12 or above on the Beaufort scale; *Force 10 from Navarone* speaks for itself; and a *High Wind* is probably a bit less again, though the novel's actual events suggest the phrase is an ironic understatement.

A10

They all have vegetable names – and might therefore have been found at London's Covent Garden Market which moved from its original site in WC2 to Nine Elms in SW8, in 1974.

The Russian is Boris **Pasternak** (1890–1960), winner of the Nobel Prize for Literature in 1958, whose name means **parsnip**. His novel *Dr Zhivago* was first published in Italy in 1957, some parts of it having been written as long as forty years earlier.

Albert R. 'Cubby' **Broccoli** (1909–96) was the Italian-American co-producer of the first James Bond film, *Dr No*, in 1962 – kick-starting one of the most successful movie franchises of all time. He oversaw production of 17 films in the series, 9 of which were co-produced with Harry Saltzman. The pair also produced the children's film *Chitty Chitty Bang Bang* (1968), also based on a book by Ian Fleming.

The German Chancellor in 1982–98 was Helmut **Kohl**, whose name means a **cabbage**. The longest-serving German leader since the war, he presided over reunification and was an energetic driving force behind wider European integration and the EU.

ROUND 8

Q1

Why would you look for treasure in an anchorite's dwelling in Russia, in offices in Italy or in an old leper colony in France?

CLUES

- All of these places are very much on the tourist trail.
- You would not have to search hard for the treasure. It is all around you, in all three places.

Q2

What do the poet who eulogized Brooklyn Bridge, a churchman who's buried beside Stella and the creator of *Briggflatts* and of overdrafts from Persia have in common?

CLUES

- These people are, respectively, an American, an Irishman and an Englishman.
- It's arguable where they would each come in the pecking order.

A1

Because they're all great art museums.

The **Hermitage** (properly the State Hermitage Museum) in St Petersburg is Russia's greatest art museum, housing a collection of some three million items in five buildings, including the world famous Winter Palace built in the 1750s.

The offices are the **Uffizi** (*Galleria degli Uffizi*) in Florence, designed in the 1560s by Giorgio Vasari, originally to house the *magistrati* or public offices of the city. As early as 1581 the top floor had become a gallery; the building now houses one of Europe's most valuable collections.

The 'leper colony' is the probable origin of the word **Louvre**, given since medieval times to the area in Paris now occupied by the vast museum of that name. It's housed in a former royal palace, which was converted to a gallery in 1793 to show off the treasures of the French kings – there having been no real call for a palace any more.

A2

All three have birds' names as a surname.

The poet who eulogized Brooklyn Bridge is Hart **Crane** (1899–1932), in his long poem of 1930, *The Bridge*.

The churchman is Jonathan **Swift** (1667–1745), whose intimate letters to Esther Johnson ('Stella') were published as *Journal to Stella*. He was buried by her side in St Patrick's, Dublin, where he was Dean.

Basil **Bunting** (1900–85) was probably the foremost Northumbrian poet of the twentieth century, who worked as a journalist on a local paper in Newcastle-upon-Tyne in the years before the publication of his most famous work, the long poem *Briggflatts* (1966). His incantatory style was heavily influenced by Ezra Pound and he published translations of poems from Latin and Persian, under the title *Overdrafts*.

Q3

What might be the vehicle of choice of Pip's lawyer acquaintance, a printer of the First Folio and the Dartford warbler?

CLUES

- Unlike in the previous question, in this instance the Dartford warbler is not a bird.
- The vehicle would be appropriate for the third but entirely anachronistic for the first two.

Q4

Explain why, and when, you could have found all of the following sailing under Hart's flag at teatime: someone who looks after horses, an ericaceous landscape, a spiced dish and the spot where they laid the Earl of Moray?

CLUES

- These four are taken from what is now a very long sequence.
- They were very often accompanied by pet animals.

A3

A Jag; because JAG are the first three letters of all three names.

The lawyer who takes Pip under his wing and administers his mysteriously sourced allowance, in Dickens's *Great Expectations*, is Mr **Jaggers**.

One of the two printers of the Shakespeare First Folio (1623) credited on the title page is Isaac **Jaggard** (in collaboration with the bookseller Edward Blount). It was Isaac's father, William Jaggard, who was given the commission for the First Folio, but his son Isaac had taken over the business by the time the book was published, and it is his name on the title page below the famous engraved portrait.

The 'Dartford Warbler' is a perhaps unkind reference to Dartford's most famous son, Sir Mick **Jagger**. Born in July 1943, he has been the lead singer of the Rolling Stones since he was 19.

A4

They all suggest the surnames of presenters on the BBC children's TV show *Blue Peter* – and they all appeared (although not all simultaneously) in the 1980s.

The famous blue-and-white ship design, recognized by generations of children as the programme's emblem, was created in 1963 by the artist and children's TV presenter Tony Hart. Sharing the studio set with them, routinely, were the show's various cats and dogs.

The four presenters suggested by the clues are: Simon **Groom** (who was with the show in 1978–86); Tina **Heath** (1979–80); Mark **Curry** (1986–9); and Sarah **Greene** (1980–3). The Moray reference is to the often-misheard folk song in which 'they have slain the Earl o' Moray and laid him on the green'. The mishearing has given rise to the coinage 'mondegreen', meaning a word or phrase that's mistaken for another, often to comical effect.

Q5

In what ways are Strauss's operatic quest, Gene Pitney's first million-selling hit and Musil's Vienna epic lacking, and what therefore connects them with *Vanity Fair*?

CLUES

- The Gene Pitney song is the theme from a film.
- Musil never actually finished his epic, but that's not the point.

Q6

What kind of tranquil location might be common to a famous daughter of Rochdale, a photographer who recorded life in North Yorkshire and a nostalgic novelist from Gloucestershire?

CLUES

- They don't share the same name, but their names have a connection.
- Nostalgia is a theme in the work of all three.

A5

They are all 'without' something.

Richard Strauss's opera ***Die Frau ohne Schatten*** (*The Woman Without a Shadow*), with a libretto by Hofmannsthal, was first performed in Vienna in 1919. The woman of the title is the Empress, a supernatural being who emerged from a white gazelle shot by the Emperor while out hunting. Because theirs is a union of human and spirit, she can bear no children, and this barrenness is symbolized by her lack of a shadow. She must undergo many trials and much subterfuge in the course of the opera in her quest to become human, acquire her shadow, and have a chance of happiness through bearing children.

The movie ***Town Without Pity*** (1961) starred Kirk Douglas as a US Army major with the unenviable task of defending four young GIs after they gang-rape a teenage girl in a German village where they're stationed. Its subject matter and unflinching treatment made it strong stuff for the time. Dimitri Tiomkin's Oscar-nominated theme song became Gene Pitney's first million seller.

Austrian novelist Robert Musil's major work is the enormous Proustian masterpiece ***The Man Without Qualities*** (*Der Mann ohne Eigenschaften*), begun in 1921 and still unfinished at his death in 1942. A detailed portrait of decadent fin-de-siècle Vienna, it contains many autobiographical elements. Musil's giant work brought him no fame or wealth; he toiled at it daily, at the expense of the need to provide for his family. But Thomas Mann admired it hugely, and Milan Kundera has cited it as one of the most important literary works of all time.

The subtitle of William Makepeace Thackeray's *Vanity Fair* (1847–8) is ***A Novel Without a Hero*** – the male characters being venal and flawed, and the principal female character who walks all over them, Becky Sharp, being more of an anti-heroine.

A6

They all have names with roughly the same bucolic connotation.

The inhabitant of Rochdale is Dame Gracie **Fields**, née Stansfield (1898–1979), singer, comedienne and film star whose wartime performances for the troops in Europe became legendary.

The photographer is Frank **Meadow** Sutcliffe (1853–1941), of Whitby, whose sometimes sentimental sepia portraits of fishing-village life are ubiquitous in the town's gift shops and galleries.

The novelist is Laurie **Lee** (1914–97), author of that most brilliant of evocations of youth, *Cider with Rosie* (and of course a lea is a meadow or field).

Q7

Why might you find a knight of the Round Table, a pioneering astronomer and a Shakespearean foot-soldier all accelerating towards the state of Michigan?

CLUES

- You'll find the foot-soldier mentioned in *Macbeth*.
- They would be heading for a particular town in Michigan, immortalized in a song.

Q8

A subdivision of an Act, several ungulates, St Clement's material and the Osmeridae. Did you sense that something was missing?

CLUES

- There is a reason why the question is in the past tense.
- Osmeridae are a family of fish, if that's any help.

A7

They all have 'Gal' at the beginning of their names so they might be accelerating to Kalamazoo.

The knight of the Round Table we have in mind is Sir **Galahad**; the pioneering astronomer **Galileo Galilei**; and the Shakespearian foot-soldier a **gallowglass** (as in 'kerns and gallowglasses', classes of Scottish soldier mentioned in *Macbeth*).

Their common element being *gal*, you might find them in Kalamazoo, Michigan (since the song claims 'I've got a **gal** in Kalamazoo').

And they'd be accelerating because the **gal** is the unit of measurement of acceleration due to gravity, equal to 1 cm per second squared.

A8

The clues should all lead to four senses – as in scene, herd (heard), felt and smelt. They are, therefore, homophones of the past tenses of verbs relating to four of the five senses. If you sensed – pun and clue (and past tense) intended – that something was missing, that something would be 'tasted', for which, as far as we know, no homophone exists.

As any playgoer or reader of Shakespeare knows, a play is subdivided into acts, and those acts are themselves subdivided into **scenes**.

Likewise, when ungulates such as cows gather together, that grouping is described as a **herd**.

The invention of **felt** has been attributed, among many others, to St Clement, who is supposed to have accidentally invented it by walking on wool for long periods to prevent blisters, and thus compressing it while also sweating into it.

That leaves **smelt**: *Osmeridae* is the Latin name for the family of small fish known as smelts (or more precisely freshwater or typical smelts, to distinguish them from related species that also bear the name). They resemble salmon but are smaller, and as a result of this are often eaten by them, which proves that imitation is not just the sincerest form of flattery, but also the surest way of getting killed.

Q9

Where might you find the following, and in what category would you group them?

CLUES

- They'd all make pretty loyal companions.
- The connection between them is a question of breeding.

Q10

What, or rather who, is the missing link between: the phone number of a hotel in New York; a small earthen receptacle; a streetcar interchange with the name of a dinner jacket; and a vigilant group of GIs?

CLUES

- The link is 'missing' in more than one sense.
- You could just say the answers, but we defy you not to hum them once you've worked them out.

A9

These people have the same name as breeds of spaniel – so the answer is at Crufts, in the gundog group.

Three of the official gundog breeds as recognized by the Kennel Club are Spaniel (Sussex), Spaniel (English springer) and Spaniel (Cocker).

Prince Harry is the Duke of **Sussex.**

British-born TV talk-show host Jerry **Springer** (b.1944) is best known for hosting *The Jerry Springer Show* since 1991. He is a former Democrat mayor of Cincinnati, Ohio, a former newsreader, a musician and the subject of *Jerry Springer: The Opera.*

Jarvis **Cocker** (b.1962) was the frontman of the British rock band Pulp, and is a writer and broadcaster.

A10

'Missing' is a pertinent word because the link is Glenn Miller, who went missing when his aircraft disappeared over the English Channel on 15 December 1944. He was, of course, presumed dead, but no plane or body was ever found. Gossip was rife for many years that he was serving breakfasts in a café in Herne Bay, or living under an alias in a French brothel, pre-dating similar rumours about Elvis by three decades.

The four titles are:

'Pennsylvania 6-5000', the phone number of the Pennsylvania Hotel in New York City – which is still the same, allowing for innovations in coding – (212) 736–5000.

The receptacle is a **'Little Brown Jug'**.

The streetcar interchange is **'Tuxedo Junction'** (a real streetcar junction in Birmingham, Alabama, which gave its name to a jazz club).

The vigilant GIs would be an **'American Patrol'**.

ROUND 9

Q1

What's the common action when you ... upset a lateral support to get a pulse? ... jumble up your bedclothes to get a dictator? ... take a turn downstairs to get a visitor?

CLUES

- The phrase 'jumble up' should give any crossword fan a clue to how this one works.
- By 'a dictator' we mean a proper name – the surname of a real historical figure.

Q2

A soft flower that signals spring, stilettos for beginners and *Penaeus monodon*: which would be hardest to handle?

CLUES

- *Penaeus monodon* is a crustacean.
- A feline cunning might be needed to solve this.

A1

These all involve swapping vowels around – that's the common action applied to all the pairs.

... upset a lateral support to get a pulse = **lintel** becomes **lentil**;

... jumble bedclothes to get a dictator = **linen** becomes **Lenin**;

... take a turn downstairs to get a visitor = **cellar** becomes **caller**.

A2

Probably the last of the three, because these are:

Pussy willow, the name given to the tiny furry catkins of smaller species of willow, whose appearance is an early sign of the arrival of spring;

Kitten heels, the name for low stilettos typically worn by teenagers to 'train' them to walk in heels;

Tiger prawns, *Penaeus monodon* being the species of large prawn found commonly in the Indian and Pacific oceans, and caught in great numbers for food. Fully grown specimens are often up to a foot long.

Q3

Take an American popular song of the 1940s, a John Irving novel, a time-travelling mechanic, a Bee Gees hit and a chicken. Where might you take them, and what's missing?

CLUES

- Work this out phrase by phrase and don't get yourself into a state.
- The Bee Gees hit we're thinking of was their first no. 1.

Q4

Why would a Club sandwich be appropriate for a collaborative seventeenth-century playwright, a reggae star who was the first to scale a British summit and a controversially tripped athlete?

CLUES

- The controversial tripping incident dates from the 1984 Olympics.
- If you could forgive a pun, we could have included a famous record label in this question.

A3

The clues point to the states of New England.

The popular song is 'Moonlight in **Vermont**', written in 1943 by Karl Suessdorf and John Blackburn and recorded by performers ranging from Jo Stafford and Les Brown & His Band of Renown to Frank Sinatra and Willie Nelson.

John Irving wrote *The Hotel* ***New Hampshire*** (1981) about the exotic and dysfunctional Berry family and their attempts to run hotels, first in America and then in Vienna.

The time-traveller is the **Connecticut** *Yankee in King Arthur's Court* of Mark Twain's 1889 novel; a mechanic who finds himself transported back to Camelot in the year AD 528 following a blow to the head.

The Bee Gees hit of 1967, their first no. 1, is **'Massachusetts'**. The full title is '(The Night the Lights Went Out in) Massachusetts'.

The chicken is the **Rhode Island** Red, one of the most recognizable of all breeds, developed in the US in the early 1900s.

So the sole missing New England state is **Maine**.

A4

These are all people named Decker or Dekker; so they form a 'triple decker', just as a classic Club sandwich does.

The best-known play of **Thomas Dekker** (1570–1632) is *The Shoemaker's Holiday* (1600). He was a prolific playwright in Shakespearean London, though the texts of many of his plays are lost. He often wrote in collaboration with contemporaries: John Ford and William Rowley on *The Witch of Edmonton*, Philip Massinger on *The Virgin Martyr* and Thomas Middleton on *The Honest Whore* and *The Roaring Girl*.

Although reggae music was popular in the UK throughout the mid-1960s, thanks to records brought to Britain by the increasing numbers of people arriving from the Caribbean which were then widely played in clubs and on radio, the first reggae disc to reach no. 1 in the British charts was 'Israelites' by **Desmond Dekker** (1941–2006) in April 1969.

Mary Decker (Slaney) (b.1958) was involved in the controversial 'tripping' incident with Zola Budd – who was running for the UK having had her application for British citizenship 'fast-tracked' ahead of the Games, following a zealous campaign by the *Daily Mail* – in the 3000-metre women's final at the Los Angeles Olympics in 1984. They became tangled and Decker was thrown onto the infield, injuring her hip and forcing her to pull out of the race. Budd was initially disqualified for obstruction, but reinstated an hour later after officials had viewed film footage.

Q5

A borough of a cosmopolitan city, a sporting club and foundations in two venerable seats of learning are distinguished by only an apostrophe. What are they?

CLUES

- The word 'distinguished' could have more than one meaning here.
- The two seats of learning are Oxford and Cambridge

Q6

Can you point out the fundamental similarity between the Geneva Bible, a satire by Washington Irving, and a classic socialist novel about painters and decorators?

CLUES

- The Geneva Bible had a popular nickname because of the way it translated a particular verse.
- There's a very popular dessert that will probably be more familiar than the Washington Irving book, and which contains the same name.

A5

Queens. The apostrophes here are even more of a minefield than usual!

Queens, New York, with no apostrophe; one of the city's five boroughs, bordering the East River at the western end of Long Island.

The sporting club is the **Queen's** Club, London W14, established in 1886 and named in honour of Queen Victoria; the relatively minor annual tennis tournament held there earns a great deal of attention because it is the last event on the circuit before the start of Wimbledon.

The two foundations are the **Queen's** College, Oxford, and **Queens'** College, Cambridge. The Oxford college was founded by Robert de Eglesfield in 1340 in honour of Queen Philippa, consort of Edward III. The Cambridge college was founded by two old Queens, namely Margaret of Anjou (wife of Henry VI) and Elizabeth Woodville, Edward IV's consort.

A6

These are all about gentlemen's nether garments.

The Geneva Bible (1560) is often referred to as the **Breeches Bible**, because of its translation of Genesis 3: 7, 'they sowed figge-tree leaves together and made themselves breeches' – as opposed to 'aprons' in the King James version.

The Washington Irving satire is ***Knickerbocker's History of New York*** (1809). Irving frequently published burlesques and satires under pseudonyms. The full title is *A History of New York from the Beginning of the World to the End of the Dutch Dynasty, by 'Diedrich Knickerbocker'* – a name which became synonymous with the descendants of Dutch settlers in America.

The classic socialist novel is ***The Ragged Trousered Philanthropists***, by Robert Noonan alias Robert Tressell (1914, first complete edition 1955). Set in the town of Mugsborough, it's one of the earliest and most affecting portraits of twentieth-century industrial working-class life, and a powerful tract against social injustice.

Q7

What's particularly even-handed about the architect of the National Monument, a house built for two Hollywood superstars and the most expensive property on the board?

CLUES

- The National Monument we're referring to is the one in Edinburgh.
- If you land on the last one, you're often in trouble.

Q8

Can you identify the similar connection between the following pairs?

Hiawatha and Kubla Khan

Matilda and Misery

Zero-zero-seven and One-zero

CLUES

- *Misery* is a title, but Matilda is not.
- The third pairing is the trickiest. One-zero has a sporting connection.

A7

These all contain the word 'fair'.

The co-architect of Edinburgh's National Monument, the Parthenon replica that overlooks the city from Calton Hill, was William Henry **Playfair** (1789–1857). He also built the National Gallery of Scotland, Surgeon's Hall and the Royal Scottish Academy, and thus had a considerable influence on the appearance of Scotland's capital.

The Hollywood house is **Pickfair**, built for Mary Pickford and Douglas Fairbanks by Wallace Neff around a hunting lodge they purchased in 1919. It was said to have the first private swimming pool in southern California. It was the focus of high-profile parties in the 1920s and every imaginable star of the jazz age was entertained there. It was demolished in the 1990s and replaced with a larger house on the same site, retaining only the original entrance gates.

The most expensive property on the (Monopoly) board is **Mayfair** – the 'dark blue' property which, if it has an opponent's houses or hotels on it, can be a feared obstacle on the final straight towards 'Go'.

A8

These are pairs of people with their names reversed.

Samuel Coleridge-Taylor (1875–1912) composed the choral trilogy *The Song of Hiawatha*, based on Longfellow's poetry, in 1898–1900; and **Samuel Taylor Coleridge** (1772–1834) wrote the poem 'Kubla Khan'. Confusingly, perhaps, another of Coleridge-Taylor's compositions was *Kubla Khan* (1906) but it's far less famous.

King Stephen of England (reigned 1135–54) had a long-running feud with his cousin Matilda, who imprisoned him for part of his reign. **Stephen King** wrote the novel *Misery* about the writer imprisoned by an obsessed fan (successfully filmed with James Caan and Kathy Bates).

John Barry performed the James Bond theme (hence 007), composed by Monty Norman, while **Barry John** was the majestic Welsh fly-half (no. 10) of the 1960s and 1970s.

Q9

If a former Olympic field athlete threw a party, why might he invite the following guests: a furious Scotsman; an optimistic South African; a Chilean musician; a supporter of the green party resident in west Africa; and a Greenlander who had to leave early?

CLUES

- The field athlete has a well-known enthusiasm for budgerigars.
- You'll need to navigate your way carefully through this question.

Q10

The author of *Anabasis*, a warrior princess, the inspiration of America's joggers and Malik El Shabazz – how might these characters help you on 14 February?

CLUES

- *Anabasis* dates back to the fourth century BC.
- All of the others are much more recent.

A9

The former Olympic field athlete Geoff Capes (b.1949) throws the party. The nationalities and personalities of the guests are clues to famous Capes on the coasts of their respective countries.

A furious Scotsman gives us Cape **Wrath**, the most north-westerly point of mainland Scotland.

An optimistic South African would suggest the Cape of **Good Hope**, Western Cape Province, first sighted by the Portuguese navigator Bartolomeu Dias in 1488.

A Chilean musician would give us Cape **Horn**, the steep rocky headland on Hornos Island, Tierra del Fuego, southern Chile. It was named Hoorn for the birthplace of the Dutch navigator Willem Corneliszoon Schouten, who rounded it in 1616.

A supporter of the green party resident in West Africa might suggest Cape **Verde**, Senegal, the westernmost point of mainland Africa.

A Greenlander who was unable to stay for very long would lead you to Cape **Farewell**, the southernmost point of Greenland, on Egger Island. Egger Island and the surrounding islands are called the Cape Farewell Archipelago.

A10

The fourteenth of February is St Valentine's Day, when people traditionally send their loved ones cards signed with x's to represent kisses. The clues give us names which all feature the character x and thus provide us with a neat line of x's.

Xenophon, the Greek soldier and philosopher (c.430–354 BC), was a disciple of Socrates. His *Anabasis* [pron. 'an-ABBA-sis'] describes how he led ten thousand Greek mercenaries on a thousand-mile march across enemy territory.

At the other cultural extreme, Lucy Lawless plays the title role in the cult TV series ***Xena**: Warrior Princess*.

Jim **Fixx** penned several bestselling manuals for joggers, which fuelled the running boom of the late 1970s and early 1980s, including *The Complete Book of Running* in 1977. His influence waned somewhat after he died of a heart attack while out jogging in 1984, aged only 52.

Malik El Shabazz was the last of the names taken by the human rights activist originally named Malcolm Little (1925-65), better known to posterity as Malcolm **X**.

ROUND 10

Q1

Coming or going, either way you'd be just as likely to encounter Magwitch's beneficiary, a collaborative Premier, a financier and economics guru, and an English writer who resurrected Hercule Poirot. Why, and who are they?

CLUES

- Magwitch is a Dickensian character.
- The Premier, it's generally accepted, was 'collaborative' in a negative rather than a constructive sense.

Q2

What biblical link connects stories by Faulkner to a world record hurdler and a naive American artist?

CLUES

- We're looking for a major biblical character who connects them all.
- The hurdler's best remembered achievements were in the 1970s and 1980s

A1

Their surnames are all palindromes, hence you'd find them the same whether they were coming (forwards) or going (backwards).

Abel Magwitch's beneficiary, the intended recipient of his fortune in Dickens's *Great Expectations*, is Philip **Pirrip** – abbreviated throughout, of course, to Pip, which is also a palindrome.

The man who led the collaborating Vichy government of France in 1942–4 was Pierre **Laval**, executed by firing squad in 1945.

The financier is George **Soros** (b.1930), Hungarian-American businessman, currency speculator and prophet of the markets.

The writer who in recent years has published a series of novels featuring the great Belgian sleuth Hercule Poirot, 40 years after Dame Agatha Christie laid him to rest, is Sophie **Hannah** (b.1971). She is an acclaimed poet and has also created another successful crime-novel series featuring detectives Simon Waterhouse and Charlie Zailer, some of which have been televised. She is the daughter of regular *Round Britain Quiz* panellist Adèle Geras.

A2

The name Moses.

Go Down, Moses is a collection of short stories by William Faulkner, which appeared in 1942.

Ed Moses (b.1955) won Olympic gold in the 400-metre hurdles in 1976 and 1984.

'Grandma Moses' (Anna Mary Robertson Moses, 1860–1961) became famous in the early twentieth century as a naive folk painter.

Q3

What might Dr Parnassus do with Molière's Argan, Soren Lorenson and the square root of -1?

CLUES

- Soren Lorenson might be familiar if you have read children's picture books in the past couple of decades.
- Don't try to work out the square root of -1. Part of the point is that you can't.

Q4

What might be the common location of all of these?

CLUES

- It will help to know the name of the strip cartoon in which the characters in the third picture appear.
- The band in the first picture is of Welsh origin.

A3

He would very likely collect them for his *Imaginarium* – as in the Terry Gilliam film *The Imaginarium of Doctor Parnassus* (2009, lead role played by Christopher Plummer) – because these are all imaginary things.

Molière's comedies often rely on the main character having one particular and exaggerated flaw or obsession, which the other characters make fun of and exploit. Many of these comic roles were played on the stage by Molière himself. The hypochondriac Argan in ***Le Malade Imaginaire*** (1673) was Molière's last role before his death – he collapsed on stage during his fourth performance as Argan, just a week after the premiere.

Soren Lorenson, as many parents of small children will know, is the **imaginary friend** of Lola in the picture books about Charlie and Lola, by the English writer and illustrator Lauren Child (b.1965).

The square root of -1 is an example of an **imaginary number**. There is no known number which, when multiplied by itself, can possibly give -1. All imaginary numbers are in fact multiples of √-1 and it is therefore often known as *i*, the **imaginary unit**. The term 'imaginary number' was coined by mathematicians in the seventeenth century and the concept was derided as pointless, but such numbers have gained a more important place in modern mathematics where they are an essential element of what are known as 'complex numbers'.

A4

You'd find them on the 'street', because all the answers feature streets as the middle element of a three-word phrase.

The band in the picture is the **Manic Street Preachers**, formed in the late 1980s in Blackwood in Caerphilly.

The **Bow Street Runners** were the first official police force of the city of London. They were established in 1749 by the novelist Henry Fielding, then a London Court Magistrate, regulating the disparate and corrupt law enforcement system that had previously operated.

The **Bash Street Kids** are probably the most famous creation of artist Leo Baxendale, who drew their adventures in the *Beano* comic from 1954 until David Sutherland took them over in the 1960s. The picture shows a commemorative UK postage stamp depicting characters from the strip, marking the 75th anniversary of the *Beano* comic.

Q5

What material connection is there between *Beowulf*, the Salem witch trials and a cry of 'Wakey-wakey'?

CLUES

- The word 'material' is, er, material to the question.
- You're looking for three people who share a name.

Q6

Which restless quintet might be associated with a second crop after the harvest, a feast for those in penury, what you'd have if you'd been making a collage, and an unappetizing-sounding broth?

CLUES

- Getting the answer to this will give you satisfaction.
- If you grew up in the 1960s you're probably at an advantage with this one.

A5

Cotton.

The only extant manuscript of the Old English poem *Beowulf* is the Cotton MS, so called because it came into the possession of the seventeenth-century manuscript collector **Sir Robert Cotton**. It was catalogued as *Cotton Vitellius A XV* (the fifteenth volume on the first shelf under the bust of Vitellius in Cotton's library). A fire at Ashburnham House in Westminster in 1731, where the Cotton collection was housed, did serious damage to the MS of *Beowulf* and also to one of the only four extant copies of Magna Carta, which was also in Cotton's collection. The Cotton collection was moved to the British Museum in the mid-eighteenth century and is now in the British Library.

Cotton Mather (1663–1728) was a New England Puritan preacher and pamphleteer whose suspicions, and writings and speeches in condemnation, of women and girls caught up in the witch trials at Salem, Massachusetts in 1692, are regarded as having greatly fanned the flames of the hysteria.

Billy Cotton (1899–1969) was best known for *Billy Cotton's Band Show* which was always introduced with his catchphrase exclamation of 'Wakey-wakey!' He set up his own dance band, the London Savannah Band, in 1924, and it featured major British jazz musicians Nat Gonella and Arthur Rosebery. 'Somebody Stole My Gal' was its theme song. Cotton toured with ENSA during the Second World War and was given his radio series in 1949. It lasted until 1968 when he became too ill to continue, and he died the following year. His son (Sir) Bill Cotton became managing director of BBC television.

A6

The 'restless' quintet is the Rolling Stones – restless because a rolling stone proverbially gathers no moss. The elements suggest four Rolling Stones album titles.

The second crop after the harvest is the ***Aftermath*** (1966) – a word now much more commonly used metaphorically.

A feast for those in penury might be a ***Beggars Banquet*** (1968).

When you've made a collage you're likely to have ***Sticky Fingers*** (1971).

Continuing the sequence, an unappetizing-sounding broth is therefore ***Goats Head Soup*** (1973).

Q7

Put the following in lyrical order and suggest which might be the odd one out: a wise person, Bing Crosby's love interest in *White Christmas*, a chronologizing magazine and an animated lion.

CLUES

- Bing's love interest is another singer.
- There's a connection with the North Yorkshire coast.

Q8

What's enlightening about a modern minimalist composer, an Irishman hanged for treason in 1916 and an Oxford college that was the last male preserve?

CLUES

- The composer is American.
- Get any one of these elements and you'll probably see the light straight away.

A7

The elements give us Parsley, Sage, Rosemary and Thyme.

Another name for a wise person is a **sage**.

Bing Crosby's love interest in the Michael Curtiz film *White Christmas* (1954) was Betty, played by **Rosemary** Clooney (1928–2002). The film features the song 'White Christmas' but Crosby first sang it in the earlier *Holiday Inn* (1942). Rosemary Clooney was George Clooney's aunt.

A chronologizing magazine would be ***Time***, created in 1923 by Briton Hadden and Henry Luce, the first weekly news magazine in the United States.

Parsley was the 'very friendly lion' in the BBC animated children's TV series *The Herbs*, created in 1968 by *Paddington* author Michael Bond. Other characters included Dill the dog, the aristocratic Sir Basil and Lady Rosemary, teacher Mr Onion and his pupils, the little chives.

These four herbs appear in this order in the lyrics to the folk song 'Scarborough Fair', recorded many times but perhaps most famously by Simon & Garfunkel on their album *Parsley, Sage, Rosemary and Thyme* (1966).

The odd one out is ***Time*** as its spelling differs from that of the herb in question.

A8

They're 'enlightening' because their names all suggest windows.

Philip Glass (b.1937) is the composer.

Roger Casement was hanged for treason in 1916 after visiting Germany to recruit help for the Irish nationalist cause.

Oriel College was the last Oxford college to admit women students (as late as 1988). An oriel window is a bay-window in an upper storey.

Q9

An annoying black fly prevalent in spring; a therapeutic yellow-flowering herb; a spell of good weather in the autumn; and a Bach masterpiece. What are they all doing in the rushes, o?

CLUES

- The final phrase is a reference to another folk song, and it may help to remember the words.
- If you're thinking 'Indian summer,' you need to find a different phrase for the same thing.

Q10

On which road might you have encountered the Dark Lady of DNA, a still superhero, London's Mercurial editor and Lassie's father?

CLUES

- In fact, these represent just four of a much larger group.
- Originally you'd have found them on horseback.

A9

They are named after the four evangelists – who crop up in the traditional song 'Green Grow The Rushes, O' in a line about 'the Gospel makers':

> **Five for the symbols at your door,**
> **Four for the Gospel makers...**

St Mark's fly, *Bibio marci*, is a quite large but harmless black fly with dangly legs which swarms and becomes a pest in Britain in late April/early May. It's so called because the feast day of St Mark is 25th April.

St John's wort, *Hypericum perforatum*, is a yellow-flowering meadow herb whose name (again) derives from the fact that it flowers around the feast day of St John, 24th June. It's used as an alternative therapy for treating mild depression.

A late spell of dry, warm weather (around St Luke's Day, 18th October) is traditionally called a **St Luke's Summer** – a term now more or less superceded by the American phrase an 'Indian summer', meaning pretty much the same.

J. S. Bach's ***St Matthew Passion***, a setting of the Latin mass first performed in 1729, is widely regarded as his greatest achievement in choral music.

A10

On the road between London and Canterbury – which was the pilgrim route to the shrine of St Thomas Becket. The people in the question share their names with four of Chaucer's pilgrims making that journey in *The Canterbury Tales*: Franklin, Reeve, Squire, Knight.

The title 'The Dark Lady of DNA' has often been applied – notably in the title of Brenda Maddox's 2002 biography – to **Rosalind Franklin**, who worked alongside Crick, Watson and Wilkins to identify the structure of DNA, but who was denied a Nobel Prize by her early death from cancer in 1958.

The still superhero is **Christopher Reeve** (1952–2004), the actor who played Superman in the 1970s and 80s, but was then paralysed in a riding accident; his autobiography was published in 1998 under the title *Still Me*, a brilliant, if slightly macabre, pun.

The literary periodical the *London Mercury* was most notable for its opposition to modernism in all its forms. It was edited by **J. C. Squire**, who was himself a poet.

Lassie's father, although obviously not in the strictly biological sense, was the writer **Eric Knight**, who created the character of the collie with a conscience in a story for the *Saturday Evening Post* in 1938.

ROUND 11

Q1

If a grumpy king of Sweden got together with *Vorombe titan*, a fiery St Erasmus and Cleveland the twenty-second and twenty-fourth, who would take the biscuit – and in which seedy area would they all live?

CLUES

- St Erasmus is also known by another name, which will help you.
- This question could take you back to your childhood.

Q2

Why might you find Julia Roberts and King Lear's daughters on a pedestrian crossing in Louisiana?

CLUES

- The names of King Lear's daughters are not going to be of any use to you.
- The names of types of pedestrian crossing in the UK might be more useful.

A1

The seedy area is Sesame Street as they all suggest characters from the long-running children's television show.

King **Oscar** II (not the Grouch) was king of Sweden in 1872–1907 (and of Norway in 1872–1905).

Vorombe titan is the largest bird known to modern science ever to have roamed the Earth – so it was a very **Big Bird**. It's the largest example yet unearthed of an elephant bird (belonging to the family *Aepyornithidae*), an extinct group of colossal flightless birds that roamed what's now Madagascar during the Late Quaternary.

St Erasmus is also known by the name **Elmo** – as in St Elmo's Fire, luminosity accompanying brush-like discharges of atmospheric electricity that sometimes appears as a faint light on the extremities of pointed objects such as church towers or the masts of ships during stormy weather, or along electric power lines. It is often taken as a good omen because it tends to appear as storms are dying out.

The twenty-second and twenty-fourth president is **Grover** Cleveland who served two discontinuous terms (1885–9 and 1893–7);

Cookie Monster, naturally, would take the biscuit.

A2

The linking word is Pelican.

The Pelican Brief is a 1993 film thriller based on a John Grisham novel published the previous year, starring Julia Roberts as a young law student and Denzel Washington as a reporter investigating the assassination of two Supreme Court justices.

King Lear, ranting in near-madness in the hovel where he encounters Edgar disguised as Tom o' Bedlam (Act III Scene iv), says:

Judicious punishment. It was this flesh begot
Those **pelican daughters**.

The reference is to the ancient belief that pelicans' young feed on the parent bird's blood.

A pedestrian crossing is a **Pelican crossing** (an abbreviation for Pedestrian Light Controlled Crossing), using a push-button that prompts the traffic lights to change to red, introduced in the UK in 1969.

Louisiana is the **Pelican State** – named because of the flocks of pelicans that inhabit the bayous on the Gulf Coast.

Q3

Hot Chocolate had one that dated from 1815; the Human League, one from 1854; and the Pet Shop Boys, one from 1864. Can you explain?

CLUES

- Kate Bush had one dating from 1847.
- Some pop stars are very well-read.

Q4

Why would eight Kings of England measure a variable electric current; a German opera composer tell you about magnetism; and a certain physical elegance be a guide to whether something is runny?

CLUES

- Measurement is important.
- The German composer, unfortunately, is not Wagner, or Strauss, or Offenbach.

A3

This is about hit songs which have the same titles as nineteenth-century novels.

Hot Chocolate had a substantial UK hit in 1974 with a song named **'Emma'**, about an actress who took her own life after failing to make the big time, and nothing whatsoever to do with the 1815 Jane Austen novel of that title.

The Human League's hit song **'Hard Times'** likewise shared nothing with the 1854 Charles Dickens novel except for its title: the 12-inch medley of that song with 'Love Action' is regarded as a highlight of their catalogue.

The Pet Shop Boys took the title of Anthony Trollope's first 'Palliser' novel ***Can You Forgive Her?*** (1864) as the title for a hit song of 1993.

(Unlike all of the above, Kate Bush's first hit 'Wuthering Heights', in 1978, took its inspiration directly from the Emily Brontë book.)

A4

These are all units of measurement in physics.

Inductance (the degree to which an electromotive force is generated in an electrical circuit by variations in the current flowing through it) is measured in **henries**, H.

Magnetic flux is measured in **webers,** Wb (the reference in the clue is to Carl Maria von Weber, 1786–1826, composer of *Der Freischütz*).

A non-SI unit measuring dynamic viscosity (which is also measured in Pascal seconds, Pa s) is called the **poise**, P. More often encountered is its subdivision the centipoise (cP), which is almost exactly equivalent to the viscosity of water at 20°C.

Q5

Why might a bark beetle make you take a stiff drink, take extra care when getting out of your car or pay your own share of the bill?

CLUES

- It's not so much the beetle itself as what it causes.
- Think about what nationality these might suggest.

Q6

A promising Texan who died at the age of 22, a character played by Burt Ward and Daenerys's killer could all be very cosy in an American university at a particular time of year. Who, where, when?

CLUES

- We're not looking for an individual university so much as a group of universities.
- The Texan is a musician.

A5

They all refer to things that are supposedly 'Dutch'.

Dutch elm disease is caused by the fungus *Ophiostoma ulmi*, spread by bark beetles, first observed in the Netherlands in 1910 and responsible for the ravaging of some 25 million native elms in the UK during the twentieth century.

Dutch courage, meaning a stiff drink, supposedly derives from the seventeenth-century Great Plague of London, when the Dutch were the only sailors prepared to sail up the Thames to supply the stricken city. They used to take a few stiff drinks to fortify themselves before putting into port. To this day, as a mark of gratitude, Dutch ships dock in the Pool of London without paying berthing fees.

A safety manoeuvre in which you get into the habit of reaching for your driver's door handle with the opposite hand – so that it forces you to turn and glance at obstacles or traffic that might be coming alongside you – is called a **Dutch reach**.

If everyone pays their own share of the bill at a meal, they '**go Dutch**'. (But just remember I didn't have a starter.)

A6

They are all related to Christmas.

The promising Texan is Buddy **Holly**, killed in a plane crash on 3 February 1959 (a date later immortalized in Don McLean's tribute song 'American Pie' as 'the day the music died').

The character played by Burt Ward was **Robin**, sidekick to Adam West's Batman in the cult TV series of the 1960s.

Daenerys Targaryen's killer, in the final series of *Game of Thrones* based on the novels by George R. R. Martin, is Jon **Snow**.

So they'd clearly be at home in an **Ivy** League university (the name given to the group of prestigious colleges on America's east coast: Princeton, Harvard, Yale, Dartmouth, Cornell, Columbia, Brown, Pennsylvania) … at **Christmas**.

Q7

If an anatomy textbook, an Inn of Court and a clownish Master of Ceremonies are three, how many more would you need to achieve a twenty-first-century publishing sensation?

CLUES

- The answer to this is more black and white than you'd think.
- The anatomy textbook may be more familiar to you as the title of a TV show.

Q8

If *Tales from Topographic Oceans* and Kan'ami and Zeami represent certainties, why is *Flora Britannica* somewhat more ambivalent?

CLUES

- Kan'ami and Zeami are Japanese historical figures.
- It's the *author* of *Flora Britannica* we're interested in rather than its subject matter.

A7

The clues are all 'grey' (or 'gray') – so if these count as 3 shades of grey, we need another 47.

British writer E. L. James (Erika Leonard)'s erotic trilogy beginning with ***Fifty Shades of Grey*** became a publishing sensation in 2012 and led to a series of movie adaptations.

The standard anatomy textbook for medical students is ***Gray's Anatomy***, first published in 1858 and originally written by Henry Gray, lecturer in anatomy at St George's Hospital Medical School in London. The hit US TV series *Grey's Anatomy* (first shown in 2005) plays on the book title but with a slight spelling variant – in reference to the lead character Dr Meredith Grey (played by Ellen Pompeo).

Gray's Inn is one of the four Inns of Court, probably founded in the late fourteenth century.

Actor and photographer **Joel Grey** (b.1932) is best known as the MC in Bob Fosse's classic 1972 film (and in the earlier Broadway production) of Kander & Ebb's *Cabaret*, based on the Berlin stories of Christopher Isherwood. His performance earned him the Oscar for Best Supporting Actor. He's the father of actress Jennifer Grey, the star of *Dirty Dancing*.

A8

One is a yes, one is a no and the other is a maybe.

Tales From Topographic Oceans is a 1973 concept album by the British prog-rock band **Yes**, often cited as the most extreme example of their drawn-out, virtuosic, some would say self-indulgent, style.

Japanese **Noh** theatre was invented and developed by Kan'ami Kiyotsugu and his son Zeami Motokiyo in the Muromachi period (the fourteenth century by the Western calendar); still performed today as part of the Japanese theatrical tradition, it usually consists of musical drama derived from traditional Japanese folk tales.

If these are the certainties, *Flora Britannica* represents something more ambivalent because it's a noted work of natural history by the writer and conservationist Richard **Mabey**.

Q9

Why might you suspect that a husband with more doors than wives, a wireless Danish king and 'The Chairman of the Board' had been in contact with *Isatis tinctoria*?

CLUES

- The husband appears in an opera.
- The *tinctoria* element in the Latin name might give you a useful hint as to what connects them.

Q10

What might connect: an Anglican cleric who became an 'Eminent' Catholic; a male soldier who became a female activist; and the Third Doctor's companion?

CLUES

- 'Eminent' is a word famously used about this person by someone else.
- The fact that there was a transformation (in the case of the first two at least) is not the point of the connection.

A9

Isatis tinctoria is the plant whose leaves make the blue dye called woad, used (according to Julius Caesar) by the ancient Britons to colour their bodies. The people in this question have nicknames which suggest that their faces are blue or partly blue.

The husband with more doors than wives is **Bluebeard**, or *Barbe-bleue*, as he first appears in Charles Perrault's *Histoires ou Contes du Temps Passé* of 1697. His story was adapted in *Duke Bluebeard's Castle*, the one-act opera by Bartók and his librettist Béla Balázs, first performed in 1918, which concentrates on Bluebeard's wife's curiosity about what lies behind the seven doors that lead away from their Castle's Great Hall. She demands that Bluebeard open each one in turn, and is unpleasantly surprised to find that each contains evidence of his past and present cruelties.

Harald Blåtand or **Bluetooth** (c.911–987) was King of Denmark from 935 and of Norway from 936, the first Christian Viking king. 'Bluetooth' itself may, disappointingly, be a mistranslation: the Danish 'Blåtand' means 'dark-complexioned', probably simply implying that he wasn't blond. He has become 'wireless' in recent years as his nickname has become synonymous with the wireless networking technology developed by the Swedish company Ericsson.

Finally, 'The Chairman of the Board' was one of several nicknames given to Frank Sinatra – another, still better-known, was **'Ol' Blue Eyes'**.

A10

Their surnames.

Cardinal Henry Edward Manning (1808–92) was one of the four subjects profiled in Lytton Strachey's iconoclastic *Eminent Victorians*, published in 1918. An Anglican for the first 40 years of his life, he was ordained a Catholic priest in 1851 and appointed Archbishop of Westminster in 1865.

The American transgender whistleblower and freedom-of-information activist **Chelsea Manning** was born Bradley Manning in 1987, and came to prominence after passing hundreds of thousands of documents to Wikileaks, among which was a considerable amount of classified and highly sensitive material relating to US military intelligence.

The British actress **Katy Manning** (b.1946) played Jo Grant, the Doctor's principal companion in *Doctor Who* during the 1971–3 seasons, opposite Jon Pertwee in the Doctor's third incarnation. Her character bowed out at the end of the iconic story 'The Green Death' having fallen in love with environmentalist Professor Cliff Jones.

ROUND 12

Q1

If you can find the key to the link between Noddy and his companions, the 'St Custards skool' dog, an exclusive address on Piccadilly and *Artemisia absinthium,* you'll realize there's an odd one out. Which?

CLUES

- If you're thinking about Enid Blyton, you need to think again.
- You'll eventually find your way out of this, even though all these elements make up quite a long sentence.

Q2

Oskar, who wouldn't grow up, and Tamino, who had a charmed life, could form an unlikely band with the hero of a modern novel that begins in Sicily and ranges across America. Why?

CLUES

- Oskar is in a novel too.
- They could be a 'band' in more than one sense.

A1

All four share their names with prisons.

'Noddy and his companions' is nothing to do with Enid Blyton but refers to the (equally loveable) Noddy Holder and the rock band **Slade**.

The 'St Custards skool' dog (in the 'Molesworth' books by Geoffrey Willans and Ronald Searle) is named **Wandsworth**, no doubt as a knowing reference to London's largest prison.

The **Albany** is an exclusive block of flats next to Burlington House on London's Piccadilly, whose residents have included Lord Byron, Lord Palmerston, Gladstone, Aldous Huxley, Graham Greene, Alan Clark and (after the men-only restriction was lifted) Dame Edith Evans. Altogether a less desirable address, Albany prison is a high security facility on the site of Albany Barracks, part of HMP Isle of Wight.

Artemisia absinthium is **wormwood**, the aromatic plant that's a traditional ingredient of vermouth and absinthe (as suggested by its taxonomic name). Wormwood Scrubs prison is in London, close to White City.

What distinguishes Slade prison from the other three is that it's **fictional**, having been invented by writers Dick Clement and Ian La Frenais (and placed supposedly somewhere near Carlisle) for the TV comedy *Porridge*.

A2

Because the works in which they appear all have titles featuring musical instruments: a drum, a flute and an accordion.

Oskar Matzerath is the hero of Günter Grass's ***The Tin Drum*** (*Die Blechtrommel*, 1959), whose growth is arrested at the time of the Nazi rise to power in Germany and doesn't begin again until after the war.

Tamino is the romantic hero of Mozart's *Die Zauberflöte* or ***The Magic Flute***. The flute protects him from many dangers en route to the heart of his beloved.

Annie Proulx's 1996 novel ***Accordion Crimes*** is the story of an accordion, made by a Sicilian, which passes from owner to owner on a strange epic journey across the USA.

Q3

Look at these people – and to 'ell with them all! Why would we say that?

CLUES

- The man in the first picture needs love.
- The third is a stage performer.

Q4

Where there's the first, there's brass. Where there's the second, there's usually a bird of some description. And a bottle of the third provoked Long John into song. So what's the fourth?

CLUES

- You might have an advantage with this question if you're a Scot.
- The question has a whiff of salt water about it, quite apart from the mention of Long John.

A3

Because they have names beginning with 'two ls'.

LL Cool J, originally James T. Smith (b.1968), who took his stage name (short for Ladies Love Cool James) when he was 16. His hits include 'I Need Love' and 'Ain't Nobody'.

Tennis star **Lleyton Hewitt** (b.1981), 2001 US Open and 2002 Wimbledon singles champion.

The English music hall singer **Marie Lloyd** (1870–1922), real name Alice Matilda Victoria Wood. At the peak of her success in the 1890s, she became known for her cheeky performances of songs such as 'My Old Man Said Follow the Van', and 'Oh Mr Porter What Shall I Do?'.

A4

These are islands off the west coast of Scotland, just south of Skye, often known collectively as the Small Isles. They appear here in rough order of distance from the mainland, so the fourth is Canna.

Where there's **Muck** there's brass.

The bird would have laid an **Eigg**.

Long John Silver's refrain in Robert Louis Stevenson's *Treasure Island* was 'Fifteen men on the dead man's chest/Yo ho ho and a bottle of **Rhum**'.

The next island, the furthest out in the group, is **Canna**.

Q5

What fate was shared by: a vivid recreation of a revolution, a treatise on natural selection, a novel about Ireland published in France and verses which were not poetry? And which is the odd one out?

CLUES

- Identifying the titles here may not be enough.
- If you can get the link here you're really on fire.

Q6

A female character in the movies who wasn't played by Julie Andrews or Natalie Wood, but had the same name, was a precursor of Klaatu's companion and a fussy interpreter. Who – or perhaps what – are they?

CLUES

- You could say we're being a little inhuman by giving you this question.
- We're in the realm of science fiction.

A5

This is about books that have been burned.

The original handwritten manuscript of Carlyle's ***The French Revolution***, vol.1, was accidentally used by a housemaid to light a fire while on loan to John Stuart Mill. Carlyle rewrote it all from memory.

Charles Darwin's ***The Origin of Species*** (full title *On the Origin of Species by Means of Natural Selection and the Preservation of Favoured races in the Struggle for Life*), published 1859, was publicly burned by Christians in the Deep South of the USA as a reaction against attempts to teach Darwin's theories in schools during the early twentieth century.

The New York post office authorities burnt the entire shipment of copies of the first English edition of ***Ulysses***, printed in Paris by Sylvia Beach, in 1922.

Protestors publicly burnt copies of Salman Rushdie's novel ***The Satanic Verses*** in anger at what they saw as the blasphemy within. The Ayatollah Khomeini of Iran issued a 'fatwa' in February 1989, from which Rushdie was officially protected at some expense to the British taxpayer. It was apparently lifted in 1998.

The odd one out is the Carlyle, which was burned by accident – the others were all burned deliberately.

A6

They are famous robots in science-fiction films.

The mad scientist Rothwang (played by Rudolf Klein-Rogge), in Fritz Lang's 1927 masterpiece *Metropolis*, constructs a robot called **Maria** who is the alter-ego of a human character of the same name played by Brigitte Helm, and who incites the workers to revolt, with disastrous consequences. This pioneering piece of silent science fiction set in a mammoth industrial system was inspired by Lang's first sight of the skyline of Manhattan in 1924. The characters played by Julie Andrews in *The Sound of Music* (1965) and Natalie Wood in *West Side Story* (1961) are, of course, also named Maria.

Klaatu's companion in the cult sci-fi film *The Day the Earth Stood Still* (1951) is a robot called **Gort**. The pair arrive in a silver spaceship in the middle of Washington, DC on a mission to warn the people of Earth to stop nuclear testing before they destroy their own planet. Michael Rennie played Klaatu, and Lock Martin the huge impassive Gort. The score is by Bernard Herrmann and the film was directed by Robert Wise who, coincidentally, later made *The Sound of Music*.

The interpreter, among the best-known movie robots of all, is **C-3PO** (See-Threepio), the fussy droid in the *Star Wars* films, played by Anthony Daniels. His role is to interpret the myriad alien languages the cast encounter in their travels through space.

Q7

What's the bond between Kylie's first no. 1 in Australia, a classic comedy set on the English Riviera and an educational institution founded for the betterment of society?

CLUES

- Kylie's first no. 1 in Australia was not her first no. 1 in the UK.
- You need to think about who *created* all of these things.

Q8

What do Brian Friel, William Blake's painting of Albion and Lou Reed have to be so cheerful about?

CLUES

- They are all associated with two-word phrases that have one word in common.
- Brian Friel is a playwright, but what you need is not the title of one of his plays.

A7

The answer would be a marital bond: this is about husband-and-wife creative partnerships.

The song with which Kylie had her first Australian no. 1 (in 1987) was 'Locomotion', originally recorded by Little Eva Boyd in 1962 and written by **Gerry Goffin and Carole King**, who were husband and wife at the time of its composition.

The comedy is *Fawlty Towers*, written between 1975 and 1979 by **John Cleese and Connie Booth**, who were also husband and wife at the time of the first series. Connie Booth played the role of Polly. Their marriage broke up in the period between the two series, which partly accounted for the four-year gap between them.

The institution is the LSE (properly the London School of Economics and Political Science), founded in 1895 by the pioneering economists and social reformers, husband and wife **Sidney and Beatrice Webb**. They had married in 1892. The idea for the LSE was conceived by the Webbs along with George Bernard Shaw and Graham Wallas at a breakfast party in Surrey in the summer of 1894, and funded by a bequest to the Fabian Society from Henry Hunt Hutchinson.

A8

They give us a Field Day, a *Glad Day* and a 'Perfect Day' – so they're having a pretty good time.

Brian Friel and actor Stephen Rea set up the **Field Day** theatre company in Derry in 1980 to produce Friel's classic play *Translations*, about the British forces in Ireland in the nineteenth century and their re-naming of ancient Gaelic places as they mapped the island for their own purposes. Field Day became a significant cultural force in Northern Ireland as a theatre group, publisher and artistic organization.

Glad Day is the name by which Blake's 1794 image of Albion, naked and raising his arms surrounded by a blaze of light, is often known. It's also called *The Dance of Albion* or *Albion Rose*. The inscription that accompanies the image reads: 'Albion rose from where he labourd at the Mill with Slaves/ Giving himself for the Nations he danc'd the dance of Eternal Death.'

'Perfect Day', a classic song from Lou Reed's 1972 album *Transformer* (produced by David Bowie), became an enormous hit when re-recorded by various artists, one line at a time, in aid of Children in Need in 1997, with the BBC Symphony Orchestra conducted by Andrew Davis. The performers included Reed himself, Tom Jones, Bono, Bowie, Dr John, Emmylou Harris, Boyzone, Thomas Allen, Lesley Garrett, Joan Armatrading and Elton John.

Q9

Why might a Christogram suggest a group of undercover British intelligence officers in Ireland, the man who wanted the Maltese Falcon back and the star of *Dr Zhivago*?

CLUES

- A Christogram is a pictorial symbol that represents Christ or Christianity.
- The bit about British officers in Ireland refers to events of a hundred years ago.

Q10

Why would Fantin-Latour be attracted by Lord Wavell's anthology, the third album by Public Image Ltd and a novel by Virginia Andrews?

CLUES

- Fantin-Latour was a French painter and it would help you to know what he painted.
- Sorry this is such a blooming hard question.

A9

The Christogram is the chi-ro, an early Christian symbol formed from the Greek letters X and P, the first two letters of the word ΧΡΙΣΤΟΣ (*Christos*). It suggests the word Cairo.

The **Cairo Gang** was a group of British intelligence officers working undercover in Ireland during the Irish War of Independence, gathering information and plotting the assassination of key republican leaders. They were probably so nicknamed because they had a habit of meeting in the Café Cairo on Grafton Street in Dublin. They were rounded up by the IRA in a series of carefully planned dawn raids and executed on 21 November 1920.

Joel Cairo is the scared little man, played by Peter Lorre, who goes to see Sam Spade (Humphrey Bogart) to ask him to recover the missing black bird, in the classic 1941 John Huston film *The Maltese Falcon*.

The star of *Dr Zhivago* (1965) was the Egyptian-born actor, racehorse owner and contract bridge player Omar Sharif (1932–2015), whose nickname early in his movie career was **Cairo Fred**.

A10

The French painter Henri Fantin-Latour (1836–1904) is best known for his meticulous studies of flowers.

His work became known to a new generation of pop-culture watchers when his piece 'A Basket of Roses' was used by graphic designer Peter Savile for the cover image on the New Order album *Power, Curruption and Lies* (1983). The other references are to works with Flowers in their titles.

Lord Wavell (Field Marshall Archibald Percival Wavell, 1st Earl Wavell, 1883–1950) was the penultimate Viceroy of India, from 1943–47, and also compiled the famous poetry anthology, ***Other Men's Flowers***, in 1944.

The Flowers of Romance was the third studio album (1981) by Public Image Ltd, the group formed around John Lydon after the break-up of the Sex Pistols.

Flowers In The Attic is a 'Gothic' novel by Virginia Andrews, credited as V. C. Andrews, published in 1979, about four children locked up by their pious grandmother in the attic of a house in Virginia for three years. It caused a stir for its treatment of incest between siblings, was banned by many US public libraries and education boards, and has been filmed twice.

ROUND 13

Q1

What would you expect RuPaul to do with an aniseed trail, a 1960s expression of disapproval, a high Reynolds number and the International Hot Rod Association?

CLUES

- This question shouldn't prove too much of a burden.
- Well done if you remember 1960s slang and know who RuPaul is …

Q2

You could turn a broadcasting regulator into a central London cultural centre and then into a glass of beer, and all just by using a little switch in the middle. Can you explain?

CLUES

- The broadcasting regulator is not Ofcom.
- With a further switch it could become a method of saving money without paying too much tax.

A1

He might recruit them for *RuPaul's Drag Race*, a TV reality competition for drag queens, which has been broadcast since 2009.

Aniseed (or some other pungent substance) is used as a substitute for the scent of the fox in **drag hunting** – when it is spread across the landscape in advance of the hunt for the hounds to follow. Drag hunting remained legal in England and Wales following the outlawing of foxhunting by the Hunting Act 2004.

In the argot of 1960s youth, something objectionable, even appalling, such as the Vietnam War, was colloquially referred to as a **drag**.

A Reynolds number is a quantity used in fluid mechanics to help predict, among other things, the **drag** on an object moving through a fluid medium

The International Hot Rod Association is one of the major governing bodies overseeing the sport of **drag racing**.

A2

This is a simple transformation of three sets of initials – IBA, ICA, IPA.

The **IBA (Independent Broadcasting Authority)** was the regulatory body for commercial television, Channel 4 and commercial radio stations in the 1970s and 1980s.

The **ICA (Institute of Contemporary Arts)** is a gallery and cultural centre on Carlton House Terrace in London, founded in 1947.

IPA (India Pale Ale) is a style of light traditional beer, which first appeared in England in the 1840s. It was regularly exported to India during the Victorian era, perhaps because one of the earliest breweries to develop the style was located very close to the East India Docks on the River Thames.

(The further switch mentioned in the clue would give you an ISA.)

Q3

Which common flower might be the emblem of Katie of Perth, Joan of Kent and Eleanor of Brittany – and why?

CLUES

- These people all go back some centuries, but they share a common sobriquet.
- Katie of Perth might strike a chord with opera buffs.

Q4

What starts to look familiar about a disease-carrying insect, a violent independence movement, spicy steamed semolina and a variety of antelope, all found in Africa; and what do they share with a famous penitentiary on another continent?

CLUES

- The penitentiary (as the use of that word might suggest) is in the USA.
- At the risk of repeating ourselves, this one really isn't too tricky.

A3

These historical figures were all nicknamed the 'Fair Maid of' somewhere.

Katie of Perth (Katherine Glover) was ***The Fair Maid of Perth***, in Sir Walter Scott's novel of that title first published in 1828 and adapted for the 1867 opera *La jolie fille de Perth* by Georges Bizet.

King Richard II's mother Joan of Kent (1328–85), wife of Edward the Black Prince, was known as the **Fair Maid of Kent**.

Eleanor (1184–1241), the granddaughter of King Henry II of England, was the **Fair Maid of Brittany**, also called the Pearl of Brittany and the Beauty of Brittany, suggesting she may have been quite attractive.

The flower that might reasonably be their emblem is the 'Fair Maid of February' – otherwise known as the **snowdrop**.

A4

Their names all consist of a short sequence of letters repeated.

The **tsetse** fly (of the genus *Glossina*) transmits nagana among cattle and sleeping sickness in humans. (It's usually pronounced 'tetsi'.)

Mau-Mau was the Kikuyu-led guerrilla independence movement in Kenya in the 1950s, from which Jomo Kenyatta emerged as the leading figure in Kenyan politics after independence.

Dik-dik is the name given to several species of dwarf antelope in the savannah lands of Africa, of the genus *Madoqua*.

Couscous is a north African dish made from steamed semolina, usually served with a hot meat sauce.

And the penitentiary on another continent is **Sing Sing** prison, at the small town of Sing Sing in Westchester County on the Hudson river, 35 miles upstream from New York City.

Q5

Why does finding the connection between DeMille's last and biggest epic, a re-telling of *The Taming of the Shrew*, and the framing of Timothy Evans lie in your own hands?

CLUES

- You might guess that the re-telling of *The Taming of the Shrew* is *Kiss Me Kate*; but you'd be wrong.
- Timothy Evans was a real person, known to people reading newspapers in Britain in the 1940s.

Q6

If you were looking to restore an old property, why might you call in Humbert Humbert, the author of *Toast* and the family at Lower Loxley?

CLUES

- You're more likely to recognize the name Lower Loxley if you're a regular BBC Radio 4 listener.
- If it's any help, the subtitle of *Toast* is *The Story of a Boy's Hunger*.

A5

The link is film titles including the number 10 (and therefore stares you in the face when you look at the fingers of both your hands).

The Ten Commandments (1956), Cecil B. DeMille's final movie, was a partial remake of his 1923 silent film of the same title. Charlton Heston starred (in his best-known role) as Moses, and Yul Brynner as his foe the Pharaoh Ramses. The vast scale of *The Ten Commandments* (particularly in the scenes of the Israelites leaving Egypt and the parting of the Red Sea), the Oscar-winning special effects, and the larger-than-life performances have made it the film for which DeMille is best remembered.

10 Things I Hate About You (1999, dir. Gil Junger) is a romantic comedy set in an American high school with a plot loosely based on *The Taming of the Shrew*. It stars Larisa Oleynik, Julia Stiles, Andrew Keegan and Heath Ledger.

10 Rillington Place (1971, dir. Richard Fleischer), about the John Reginald Christie–Timothy Evans murder case in the 1940s and based on a book about the case by Ludovic Kennedy, is named after the house in Notting Hill where the crimes occurred. Richard Attenborough starred as the devious mass murderer, and John Hurt as the simple-minded man framed and hanged.

A6

Because they all have names suggesting trades involved in building and restoration.

The part of the predatory Humbert Humbert in Stanley Kubrick's 1962 film of Vladimir Nabokov's *Lolita* was played by James **Mason**.

Toast is the 2004 memoir by the food writer Nigel **Slater**, filmed in 2010 with a screenplay by Lee Hall, and adapted for a stage play in 2018.

The family who live at Lower Loxley – in BBC Radio's *The Archers* – are the **Pargetters**. These days they consist of widow Elizabeth (née Archer) and her children Freddie and Lily, struggling to cope with life after dad Nigel fell to his death from a loose bit of roof in the show's sixtieth anniversary episode in 2011. Pargetting is decorative plasterwork most typically found in the architecture of East Anglia.

Q7

Something offered to John Keats by a much later poet, a Surrealist German rock band and the second name of a notable Globetrotter might prove the truth of the title of a kind of autobiography by a reluctant Evangelical. Can you explain?

CLUES

- The offering to Keats refers to the title of a poem, written in the 1980s.
- The rock band might send you to sleep.

Q8

An inanimate espionage agent in the Second World War who misled the enemy and made a heart-breaking story, can be linked to Lieutenant Kije and the Urban Spaceman. How?

CLUES

- The Second World War incident is a real event …
- … although there is a sense in which all of this is fictional.

A7

Citrus fruits are the link.

'A **kumquat** for John Keats' is a poem by Tony Harrison published in 1981. In it the poet speculates what Keats, supreme poet of sensual expression, would have made of the combination of bitterness and sweetness in a kumquat, had he ever had the opportunity to taste one.

Tangerine Dream was a German electronic band formed in 1967. Their founder Edgar Froese was part of Salvador Dalí's entourage in Spain for two years in the 1960s, taking part in various Surrealist 'concerts' at Dalí's villa. Froese originally viewed Tangerine Dream as a further expression of his Surrealist ideas.

Meadowlark **Lemon**, 'the Clown Prince of Basketball', was a leading member of the world-famous Harlem Globetrotters basketball team, concerned less to be taken seriously as sportsmen than to provide entertainment. They were the subjects of a popular 1970s American cartoon series, also shown in the UK. Other notable team members have included Reece 'Goose' Tatum and Wilt 'the Stilt' Chamberlain.

Together they might go to prove the truth of the title ***Oranges Are Not the Only Fruit***, the semi-autobiographical novel by Jeanette Winterson published in 1985. In it she draws heavily on her experiences as an orphaned child brought up by strict Pentecostal Evangelists in Accrington, Lancs. After preaching and saving souls at the age of 12, she rebelled in adolescence, had lesbian affairs, and drove an ice-cream van for a couple of years before leaving for a new life in Oxford and London. When she published her novel she received a note from her adoptive mother reading simply: 'You are the child of the Devil. Love Mother.'

A8

They are linked by fabrication.

The espionage agent is ***The Man Who Never Was***, in the 1955 film of that name (dir. Ronald Neame). It was based on a true incident from the Second World War in which MI6 deposited the corpse of a Marine officer in a submarine off the Spanish coast and planted on him documents giving false information on Allied plans, for the enemy to find. Duff Cooper also included the story in his novel *Operation Heartbreak* (1950).

Lieutenant Kije, in the story on which Prokofiev based an orchestral suite, is another character whose **existence was entirely fabricated**. Due to a clerical error, an ink blot was misinterpreted as referring to a non-existent Lieutenant Kije; after which it became impossible for anyone to protest that there was no such person. Prokofiev's music was written in 1934 for a film which was never completed.

And the Urban Spaceman, creation of Neil Innes and the Bonzo Dog Doo Dah Band in their hit song of 1968, provides the common link in its famous punchline: 'I'm the urban spaceman, baby, here comes the twist ... ***I don't exist***.'

Q9

What name pops up through the centuries to link an Italian humanist in the sixteenth-century English court, an inventor of horrific tales at a nineteenth-century gathering of literary talents in Switzerland and a twentieth-century record label?

CLUES

- The name appears in a slightly different form each time.
- The record label's logo features a design representing the top half of a vinyl record.

Q10

Though he may not realize it, the Duke of Edinburgh shares common beginnings with the following: an amulet used in Judaism; the arrangement of leaf-growth on a plant; and a character who became a nightingale. Why?

CLUES

- The character who became a nightingale is from classical myth.
- The link is *not* that they all originated in Greece.

A9

The name, more or less, is Polydor.

Polydore Vergil (1470–1555) was a humanist historian, friend of Thomas More, and writer of a 26-volume *History of England* which was made compulsory reading in English schools in the Tudor era. Vergil was thus an indelible influence on other historians such as Holinshed, and by extension on Shakespeare since Holinshed was Shakespeare's principal source for many of his history plays.

Dr John Polidori, a friend of Lord Byron and the Shelleys, was their companion on the shores of Lake Geneva during an extraordinary house party in the summer of 1816. Holed up in the house because of the poor summer weather, they were forced to make their own entertainment by making up horror stories with which to scare one another. This was the creative crucible that produced *Frankenstein* (the gathering was described by Mary Shelley in the original introduction).

Polydor Records, originally a German-based record label, was the first to release material by Jimi Hendrix (and, unwittingly, the first to record the Beatles, when they were total unknowns in Hamburg in 1961).

A10

Prince Philip shares the first syllable of his name with the other clues, which all begin with phil- or phyl-.

The **Phylactery** is a charm or amulet worn by orthodox Jews during morning prayer, containing Hebrew texts on folded parchments.

The pattern of leaf-growth on a plant is determined by a process called **phyllotaxis**.

The character, in Greek legend, who was turned into a nightingale was **Philomela** (or Philomel). She was raped by Tereus, king of Thrace, and her tongue was cut out so she couldn't tell anyone. But she revealed the crime by weaving a tapestry robe in which the rape was depicted, and sending it to Tereus' wife Procne. The gods turned all three of them into birds: Tereus into a hawk, Procne into a swallow and Philomela (literally 'lover of song') into a nightingale.

ROUND 14

Q1

Why could a troublesome royal cousin with imperial connections and a little girl surrounded by stupid adults find themselves hymned by a jolly swagman?

CLUES

- The jolly swagman should bring a well-known song into your head.
- The little girl appears in a book, and on stage.

Q2

Talking about your toasted brunch while wrapped in a cosy cotton blanket might lay you open to accusations of meaningless verbosity. Why?

CLUES

- We're looking for a single word with varied meanings or applications.
- You could just talk for the sake of talking until the word occurs to you.

A1

Because they are named Matilda, and the jolly swagman is the character in the traditional Australian song who sings 'Waltzing Matilda' while waiting for his billy to boil. (Originally it's thought the Matilda of the title referred to a type of knapsack rather than a girl.)

Matilda was the cousin of King Stephen of England and the daughter of Henry I, who pressed her claim to the English throne throughout Stephen's reign (1135–54). She was the former wife of the Holy Roman Emperor. After seizing London and being driven out, she eventually gave up her claim and returned to Normandy; but her son took the throne on Stephen's death, reigning as Henry II.

Matilda, in Roald Dahl's novel of the same name (1988) – adapted for an enormously successful stage musical with book by Dennis Kelly and music and lyrics by Tim Minchin – is a particularly (indeed, supernaturally) bright child who has to put up with stupid grown-ups.

A2

Because it would all be waffle.

A waffle is a kind of shaped, **toasted pancake**, especially popular as a substantial breakfast or brunch, cooked on a waffle iron so it's crisp on the outside and fluffy inside, and usually served with sweet or savoury toppings, such as chocolate and banana or smoked salmon and scrambled eggs.

The grid pattern of a waffle also gives its name to a type of **soft cotton weave blanket**.

And waffle is also, of course **meaningless verbiage**.

Q3

What pattern might the following all display: one who is fit to be loved; Scrooge; Mrs Behn's royal slave; and the red rock that used to be Henry's?

CLUES

- As with Q1, there's an antipodean connection here.
- The pattern is verbal, rather than decorative.

Q4

What might a philanthropist with an aversion to Mondays, the Goons' harmonica player and all of the inhabitants of Arnhem do to a horse?

CLUES

- The reference to Arnhem is not to *A Bridge Too Far*, though that's the right Arnhem.
- The philanthropist is not noted for being publicity-shy.

A3

They are all names containing just one vowel, repeated several times.

The name **Amanda** means 'fit to be loved';

Scrooge's first name, in Dickens's *A Christmas Carol* (1843), was **Ebeneezer**.

Oroonoko, *or the History of the Royal Slave* was the best known piece of writing by Mrs Aphra Behn (1640–89), writer and spy. It's an account of the life of a slave in Surinam inspired by a visit the author made there, and is remarkable for being one of the earliest novels in English, one of the most important written works by an Englishwoman before the nineteenth century, and one of the earliest published pleas against the slave trade.

The Australian landmark formerly known as Ayers Rock, in Northern Territory, is now officially known by its aboriginal name of **Uluru**. It's the largest individual rock mass in the world, made of sandstone containing particles of quartz and feldspar, measuring 335 m (1,110 feet) high and 9 km (6 miles) around. It was named Ayers Rock in 1873 by the explorer William Gosse, after Henry Ayers, the premier of South Australia at the time.

A4

They might geld it – because they all begin with the letters Geld.

Bob **Geldof** KBE (b. 1954) still prefers to describe his primary activity as rock singer rather than philanthropist. His biggest worldwide hit was the Boomtown Rats' 'I Don't Like Mondays' in 1979, the story of Brenda Spencer, a 16-year-old girl in Cleveland, Ohio, who perpetrated a random high-school shooting all-too-often imitated in more recent years.

Max **Geldray** (originally Max van Gelder, 1916–2004) was the Dutch-born harmonica player and comedian known to millions of BBC radio listeners in the 1950s and 1960s for his appearances on *The Goon Show.*

Arnhem is the principal city of the ancient province of the eastern Netherlands known as **Gelderland**, the provenance of the Guelders.

Q5

Can you explain why these pictures constitute a question about pictures?

CLUES

- It doesn't matter which church this is in the third picture.
- A correct answer to this is surely on the cards.

Q6

Why are the following people short of a job – but only just? The pirate Blackbeard; a special envoy who became a hostage; and a Dutch goalkeeper who played for Aston Villa and Wolves?

CLUES

- The goalkeeper's career is in the twenty-first century.
- Knowing Blackbeard's real name will help you.

A5

Because they depict Dr Martin Luther King, the rock band Queen and the nave of a church – and the king, queen and knave are the picture cards in a standard pack of playing cards.

A6

Because their names are one letter short of the name of a trade or profession.

Blackbeard's real name was Edward **Teache**, though according to some sources his birth name was Drummond. Born in Bristol, he became a privateer during the War of the Spanish Succession and subsequently terrorized ships in the Caribbean in the early eighteenth century from his 40-gun warship *Queen Anne's Revenge*. He was shot and beheaded in 1718. Teache's Hole, Ocracoke Island, North Carolina, is supposed to be his final resting place and is the site of a museum to him.

Terry **Waite** (b.1939) was captured in Beirut in 1987 while on a mission as special envoy to the Archbishop of Canterbury (then Dr Robert Runcie) to track down British and other European hostages, and was imprisoned for four years.

Stefan **Postma** (b.1976), 6 ft 7 in tall, was signed to Aston Villa by Graham Taylor for £1.5 million when Peter Schmeichel departed in 2002. He subsequently made 25 appearances for Wolverhampton Wanderers before returning to the Netherlands in 2006 to play for ADO Den Haag.

Q7

What does Elvis Presley's first no. 1 have to do with the daughter of a president, the founder of the Zoological Society of London and a cabbage?

CLUES

- The president is a former, not a current, president.
- This question takes us to three different continents.

Q8

One of America's foremost women poets might be depicted holding a bridle; the composer of 'Lullaby of Birdland', a pair of wool clippers; and a great theoretical physicist, jesses. Why?

CLUES

- None of these people is still alive.
- Jesses are pieces of equipment used by people who handle birds of prey.

A7

They are all hotels, and Elvis Presley's breakthrough recording and his first no. 1 in the US and UK was 'Heartbreak Hotel'.

Chelsea Clinton (b.1980), the only child of Bill and Hilary Clinton, is named after 'Chelsea Morning', a song by the Canadian folk singer Joni Mitchell – the song in turn having been inspired by the **Chelsea Hotel**, the downbeat Manhattan hotel where many hippies and rock stars gravitated in the 1960s. Sex Pistol Sid Vicious died there in 1979.

The founder and first president of the London Zoological Society in 1826 was Sir Stamford **Raffles**, who gave his name to the world-class hotel in Singapore, the colony he established.

A type of cabbage is a **Savoy** – also a famous hotel in London, founded by the theatre impresario Richard D'Oyly Carte, opened in 1889 and built with income from Gilbert and Sullivan's operas staged at the adjacent Savoy Theatre.

A8

Because they are Laura Riding, George Shearing and Stephen Hawking, and their names might double as the titles of portraits of them in those poses.

Laura Riding (1901–91) was one of America's most celebrated and original poetic voices of the twentieth century, who spent much of her life away from the US (in Mallorca and England) before returning there in 1959 to live in Florida. She was a literary collaborator (and lover) of Robert Graves, and Classical mythology and literature often inform her work. She also wrote criticism and fiction.

Sir George Shearing (1919–2011), blind from birth, was one of the UK's foremost jazz musicians who worked extensively in the US and composed hundreds of tunes including the standard 'Lullaby of Birdland'. He was knighted in 2007.

Stephen Hawking (1942–2018) was Lucasian Chair of Mathematics at Cambridge University. His work on black holes from 1974 onwards is fundamental to the modern understanding of the universe. He gave his name to Hawking radiation (the sub-atomic particles theoretically emitted from black holes until they cause the black hole to evaporate). He was diagnosed at the age of 21 with amyotrophic lateral sclerosis, a form of motor neurone disease.

Jesses are the straps of leather, silk or other material fastened around the legs of hawks, sometimes with leashes attached, when they are used for hunting.

Q9

What has a motto, which might be said to translate as 'I'm all right Jack', got to do with the Watergate affair and the American flag?

CLUES

- It's a musical connection we're after.
- Humming the Monty Python theme could give you a very useful hint.

Q10

Where might half an orang-utan and Leontes's daughter be spotted, along with 99 others?

CLUES

- Ask yourself how many there are altogether, and you should be well on your way to the answer.
- You'll really howl if you don't get this.

A9

The connection is the American composer of marches, John Philip Sousa.

Semper fidelis, the Latin motto which strictly means 'Always faithful', is often abbreviated (for example by the US Marines) as *semper fi* – and has come to be used in an ironic way to mean 'Screw you, Johnny, I've got mine!' or, in more British language, 'I'm all right Jack.' 'Semper fidelis' was also the title of a march by Sousa.

As was the **'Washington Post March'** – the *Washington Post* of course being the paper whose investigative reporters Bob Woodward and Carl Bernstein uncovered the Watergate scandal.

And another march by Sousa is called **'Stars and Stripes Forever'**.

(Sousa's march the 'Liberty Bell' is best known as the theme from *Monty Python's Flying Circus*.)

A10

The operative word here is 'spotted' – the clues give us the two lead canine characters in the Disney film of Dodie Smith's *One Hundred and One Dalmatians*: Pongo and Perdita.

One Hundred and One Dalmatians (1956) became a classic Walt Disney film in 1961. The iconic villainess Cruella De Vil, with fur coat and cigarette-holder, was said to have been inspired by Gloria Swanson's performance in *Sunset Boulevard* (1950). A live-action remake in 1996 featured Glenn Close as Cruella De Vil.

The two (severely endangered) species of orang-utan belong to the genus **Pongo** – the Bornean orang-utan being *Pongo pygmaeus* and the Sumatran *Pongo abelii*. The word orang-utan means 'man of the forest'.

In Shakespeare's *The Winter's Tale*, King Leontes and Queen Hermione's daughter is **Perdita**. In the play she is abandoned as a baby by the jealous Leontes who refuses to believe she is his child. The action finds her in Bohemia at the age of 16, having been brought up as a simple shepherd girl. The name Perdita is Latin for 'lost'.

NB These names refer to the film versions only, as Pongo's other half in the novel is called Missis. (Perdita does appear in the book, but in a lesser role.)

ROUND 15

Q1

Where would it get us, if we adopted an early interpretation of quantum mechanics, made promises about sovereignty and human rights, and started sympathizing with those holding us captive?

CLUES

- You need three specific phrases that relate to those descriptions.
- Pack some warm clothing.

Q2

A female traveller and mystic of fourteenth-century England shares something with a comic actor in Shakespeare's company, a twentieth-century conductor and a fictional ghost. What?

CLUES

- Only the ghost is fictional, the others were real people.
- The actor appears as a character in both the TV sitcom *Upstart Crow* and the film *Shakespeare in Love*.

A1

To northern Europe – specifically, to three capital cities.

The interpretation of quantum mechanics formulated by physicists Niels Bohr, Werner Heisenberg and others in the 1920s is known as the **Copenhagen interpretation**. It's an attempt to explain why quantum mechanics appears to contradict many of the principles of classical physics. The interpretation is not clearly defined anywhere and doesn't have a single text or a set of rules associated with it; but it forms the basis of what the majority of students have been taught about quantum mechanics ever since.

Thirty-five world leaders signed a declaration in Helsinki in 1975 advocating human rights and respect for the sovereignty of states and the self-determination of peoples – in an attempt to improve relations between Western and communist blocs in Europe. The principles agreed were known as the **Helsinki accords** or **Helsinki declaration**. It had no legal status.

When prisoners start sympathizing with, even feeling affection for, their captors, they are displaying the psychological condition called **Stockholm syndrome** – sometimes known as capture-bonding. It's named after an incident at the Kreditbanken in Stockholm in 1973, when a number of bank employees were held hostage, but became emotionally attached to their captors during the six-day siege and later defended their behaviour.

A2

The answer is the name Kemp, with or without an 'e' on the end.

Margery Kempe is the English mystic whose *The Boke of Margery Kempe* is something of a fourteenth-century classic.

The Shakespearean actor is **Will Kemp**, who starred in many comic roles with the Chamberlain's Men at the turn of the seventeenth century.

The conductor is **Rudolf Kempe** (1910–76), principal conductor and later artistic director of the Royal Philharmonic Orchestra in the 1960s and 1970s.

And the fictional ghost is **Thomas Kempe** in the 1973 children's novel *The Ghost of Thomas Kempe* by Penelope Lively.

Q3

One little boy suffered the arrows of public disapproval; 40 years later, up the street, another caused a tempestuous outcry. But a third, a different city's 'oldest citizen', goes much further in his show of defiance. Who are they?

CLUES

- All of these little boys are still with us, but none of them has grown up.
- One of them has a particular association with the BBC.

Q4

Pair a Roman soldier shot through with arrows and a Gothic wanderer. What's the link with *Swallows and Amazons* and Prince Charming?

CLUES

- This is a tough one: we're looking for a pseudonym used by a historical figure.
- Whose *voice* do you hear when you think of Prince Charming?

A3

They are three statues of boys which have offended public morals.

Alfred Gilbert's statue popularly known as **Eros**, actually thought to depict Anteros, with wings and bow and arrow, was erected in Piccadilly Circus in London in 1893 atop the fountain memorial to the Victorian philanthropist Lord Shaftesbury, one of the prime movers of nineteenth-century poor relief. The statue caused a scandal, despite the intention to symbolize Shaftesbury's selfless love for the young and unfortunate.

Ariel, sculpted by Eric Gill, was installed on the front of the newly completed BBC Broadcasting House (about half a mile up Regent Street from Piccadilly Circus) in 1933. The cloaked figure of Prospero stands behind him. The dissemination of wisdom and magic by a fleet-footed spirit of the air was considered an appropriate symbol of the fledgling broadcasting industry. His nakedness too caused a furore, and indignant questions were asked in the Commons about the sculpture's potential effect on public morality.

The **'mannequin pis'** fountain just off the Grande Place in Brussels was designed in bronze by Jerôme Duquesnoy and erected in 1619. He's fondly referred to by the populace as *le plus vieux citoyen de Bruxelles*. Legend has it that his merry urination is a symbol of the defiant independence of spirit of the city and its inhabitants.

A4

This is about Oscar Wilde.

The Roman soldier is **Sebastian**, martyred in AD 288 under the Emperor Diocletian for espousing Christianity.

The wanderer is **Melmoth**, from the Gothic novel *Melmoth the Wanderer* by Charles Maturin (1820).

Sebastian Melmoth was the wry pseudonym adopted by Oscar Wilde as he travelled Europe in 1898–1902 following his release from Reading Gaol. His final bill, from the Hotel d'Alsace in Paris where he was staying when he died, is made out to 'Monsieur Melmoth'. It was settled by his loyal long-time friend Robbie Ross.

The first ever biography of Oscar Wilde, published in 1912, was by **Arthur Ransome** – best known for his children's stories of which *Swallows and Amazons* is the first and most famous.

Wilde was recently portrayed on stage and on film by the British actor and writer **Rupert Everett,** first in the play *The Judas Kiss* (1998) and then in the movie *The Happy Prince* (2018), which he wrote and directed. Another of Everett's best known film roles is as the suave voice of Prince Charming in the second and third *Shrek* films.

Q5

Which three items emerging from a single conflict in history might mean it could justifiably be referred to as the Cold War?

CLUES

- It was, famously, fought in very cold conditions.
- The three items are familiar to us even today.

Q6

A lighthouse keeper's daughters and a journalist played by Kirk Douglas might have agreed that love is a many-splendored thing, whether they were high or low. Why?

CLUES

- See if you can get this all in one go.
- 'Love Is a Many-splendored Thing' is a song title.

A5

This is about the Crimean War, which was fought in famously perishing conditions, and which has no fewer than three separate items of warm clothing named after people or events associated with it.

The **Raglan sleeve** – cut right up to the neckline with no shoulder seam – was named after Fitzroy Henry James Somerset, 1st Baron Raglan (1788–1855), commander of British forces in the Crimea from 1854.

The **Balaklava helmet** was named after the Battle of Balaklava (also spelt Balaclava), which took place six miles from Sebastopol on 25 October 1854, the scene of the foolhardy Charge of the Light Brigade.

The **cardigan** is named after James Thomas Brudenell, the notoriously bad-tempered 7th Earl of Cardigan (1797–1868), who led the Charge of the Light Brigade at Balaklava. Despite the battlefield fiasco, he was treated as a hero on his return home.

A6

These are all Aces.

The **Ace Sisters**, Jessica Ace and Margaret Wright, the daughters of the Mumbles lighthouse keeper Abraham Ace, performed many rescues of shipwrecked sailors and are commemorated by a blue plaque noting their especially heroic rescue of the crew of the Mumbles lifeboat in 1883. Like their predecessor Grace Darling on the Northumberland coast 45 years earlier, they became internationally known through romanticized media accounts and folk songs.

The 1951 film by Billy Wilder, featuring Kirk Douglas, was ***Ace in the Hole***. Douglas played a newspaperman with a gift of a story guaranteed to get him high circulation: a man stuck down a shaft. The film centres on the highly unethical decision to delay his rescue in order to keep the story hot.

'Love is a Many-splendored Thing' was the biggest hit song (in 1955) of the American singing quartet the **Four Aces**. It was used in a movie of the same title (and won an Oscar as Best Original Song of its year), and also in a US television soap opera based on the movie.

Q7

Why, if you're arrested in the USA, might you remember an inn, or a sorcerer's innocent daughter, or a moon of Uranus?

CLUES

- This is another question about a name that's common to all of these elements.
- Moons of Uranus tend to have Shakespearean connotations.

Q8

Why might a schoolboy in a Benjamin Britten opera, a person from Jamaica, a politician derided as unkempt and a ruined abbey in County Down be regarded as imperial?

CLUES

- The politician is a British post-war figure, no longer with us.
- It might not take you long to get the measure of this question.

A7

Because police officers making arrests in the US are required by law to read the 'Miranda Rule' to the suspect – concerning their rights to remain silent, to representation by a lawyer, etc. It's so called because of Ernesto A. Miranda of Arizona, whose conviction for rape was reversed by the Supreme Court in 1966 after it emerged he hadn't been read his rights on arrest. The other references are other Mirandas.

'Do you remember an inn, **Miranda**' is the first line of Hilaire Belloc's poem 'Tarantella' (1923), and recurs as a refrain several times in the poem.

Miranda is the daughter of Prospero in Shakespeare's *The Tempest*.

One of the moons of Uranus is named **Miranda**, after the Shakespearean character. Also known as Uranus V, it's the fifth-largest of the planet's moons. Several of Uranus's moons are named after characters in *The Tempest*.

A8

Because they give us the imperial measurements miles, yard, foot and inch.

Miles and his sister Flora are the children pursued by the spirits of Peter Quint and Miss Jessel in Benjamin Britten's 1954 opera *The Turn of the Screw*, based on the Henry James ghost story of 1898.

Yardie is Jamaican expatriate slang for a person from Jamaica, probably deriving from the 'yard', the focus of social interaction in the poor suburbs of Kingston. Bob Marley's song 'No Woman No Cry' refers to recollections of 'the government yard in Trenchtown'.

The British Labour politician and writer Michael **Foot** (1913–2010) was given rough treatment by the British tabloid press, especially at the time of his leadership of the party in 1980–3, finding himself nicknamed Worzel Gummidge for his somewhat informal dress at public events.

The castle in County Down is **Inch** Castle, on the banks of the River Quoile near Downpatrick.

Q9

Why might Moira Shearer be an appropriate cheerleader for the Yankees' bitterest rivals? Which American film actor might join her? And which fairy-tale heroine might you employ to set off the ensemble?

CLUES

- These people appear, in a sense, in ascending order.
- We could easily have included a Butlin's entertainer as one of the group.

Q10

A popularizer of civilization and an admirer of ankles; a painter of dancers in Montmartre and a maker of films; and an Eminent Victorian and a beached poet. Why might they all have attracted the attention of Turgenev?

CLUES

- The pairs of people in the descriptions all bear the same relationship to one another.
- If we had given you Civilisation, with a capital C and an 's', it might have been easier.

A9

They could all provide red items for an outfit of clothing.

Moira Shearer (1926–2006), actress and dancer, took the lead role in the Powell and Pressburger film of the Frederick Ashton ballet, *The* ***Red Shoes*** (1948).

The Boston **Red Sox'** rivalry with the New York Yankees is almost certainly the keenest in Major League baseball. For much of the twentieth century the popular legend was that the team had been cursed since it sold its biggest star Babe Ruth (nicknamed 'the Bambino') to the Yankees in 1920. After 86 fallow years, the Red Sox became the first team to win four World Series titles in the twenty-first century, winning in 2004, 2007, 2013 and 2018.

Red Buttons (1919–2006) was an American character actor with credits including *The Poseidon Adventure* (1972), *They Shoot Horses, Don't They* (1969), *Stagecoach* (1966), *Pete's Dragon* (1977), *The Longest Day* (1962) and a part in the 1980s soap *Knots Landing.*

And **Red Riding Hood** might cap off the outfit.

A10

Because they are fathers and sons – and Ivan Turgenev wrote the novel *Fathers and Sons* (1862).

Kenneth Clark, later Lord Clark (1903–83), wrote and presented what is still the best-known British TV series about art history, *Civilisation*. (The BBC made an updated, more multi-cultural series entitled *Civilisations*, with various presenters, some 50 years later.) The racy political diaries of son **Alan Clark** (1928–99), published in 1993, contain confessions of numerous indiscretions and infidelities, including a notorious passage in which, sitting in the House of Commons beside Prime Minister Margaret Thatcher, he notices how attractive her ankles are.

Pierre-Auguste Renoir (1841–1919) was one of the founders of the Impressionist movement; his *Bal au Moulin de la Galette* (1876), depicting dancers and revellers at the Moulin de la Galette on the hill of Montmartre, is one of his most famous pictures, and is in the Musée d'Orsay in Paris. His son **Jean Renoir** (1894–1979) was a pioneer of realist cinema, his best known works being *La Grande Illusion* (1937) and *La Règle du jeu* (*The Rules of the Game*, 1939).

Thomas Arnold (1795–1842), headmaster of Rugby School, was profiled by Lytton Strachey in his irreverent study *Eminent Victorians* (1918). His son, the poet and critic **Matthew Arnold** (1822–88), wrote 'Dover Beach', one of the most famous expressions of Victorian uncertainty in the face of assaults on the tenets of faith.

ROUND 16

Q1

Why would you be well advised to avoid the Oscar-winning Mr Lee, an album (and accompanying film) by Harry Nilsson and Sheffield United?

CLUES

- Working out RBQ questions can sometimes be painful.
- Mr Lee is a writer/director, not an actor.

Q2

You could get 8 out of 10 for connecting Hockney's Percy, Tennessee's frustrated wife in Mississippi and what Eliot's street lamp said. How?

CLUES

- You could say this is one of our pet questions.
- We could also mention someone with whom Batman has a love-hate relationship.

A1

Because they all have the names of sharp objects.

The Oscar-winning Mr Lee is **Spike** Lee, director of acclaimed movies including *She's Gotta Have It* (1986), *Do the Right Thing* (1989), *Jungle Fever* (1991) and *BlacKkKlansman* (2018), for which he won the Academy Award for Best Adapted Screenplay.

The Nilsson album (dating from 1970) is ***The Point!***, a narrative fable with music about a round-headed boy growing up in a land where everyone and everything else is pointed. An accompanying animated film incorporating the music from the record was originally narrated by Dustin Hoffman, though for contractual reasons it was re-voiced for later releases.

Finally Sheffield United FC are nicknamed the **Blades** – because of the long history of cutlery manufacture in the city.

A2

They all refer to cats. Originating in a cat-food commercial, the phrase '8 out of 10 cats' has become so familiar in the context of marketing surveys that it has given its title to a TV panel show.

David Hockney painted ***Mrs and Mrs Clark and Percy*** in 1970–1, depicting fashion designer Ossie Clark and his wife Celia Birtwell shortly after their marriage. Percy is their cat – although, in fact, the white cat sitting on Ossie's knee in the picture is not Percy at all, but another of their cats, Blanche.

Tennessee Williams's play *Cat on a Hot Tin Roof* (1955) is about the tensions that rise to the surface at a gathering of the cotton-rich Pollitt family in Mississippi, especially those between Brick and his wife **'Maggie the Cat'**. The role was created on Broadway by Barbara Bel Geddes who, two decades later, played the matriarch in *Dallas*. The play was filmed in 1958 with Elizabeth Taylor in the role.

In several of T. S. Eliot's early poems (in the 1917 collection *Prufrock and Other Observations*), cat-related imagery recurs, for example to represent creeping fog. In the poem 'Rhapsody on a Windy Night' the street-lamp says **'remark the cat which flattens itself in the gutter'**. Phrases from this and other early poems by Eliot were adapted by Trevor Nunn for the lyrics to the song 'Memory' in the Andrew Lloyd Webber musical *Cats*.

Q3

Identify this bunch: a family who kept 3/4 time; one of a trio of fishy publishers; and the author of *Mythologiques* who might make you think of denim.

CLUES

- Think this through and don't put your head in the sand.
- You're looking for a name common to all three.

Q4

Woody Allen in 1972; Bryan Singer in 1995; Ray Bradbury in 2009: what did they all do, and which is the odd one out?

CLUES

- This is about the creative output, rather than the lives, of the people named.
- You *must* remember this …

A3

They're all called Strauss, which is the German for 'bunch'. (It also means an ostrich, often in the compound *Vogel-Strauss*.)

The **Strauss** family of Vienna (Johann I, 1804–49, and his sons Johann II, 1825–99, and Josef, 1827–70) were especially known for their waltzes (Johann II was 'the Waltz king') which are typified by a time signature of 3/4.

Farrar-**Strauss**-Giroux is the American publishing house whose logo consists of three stylized fish.

Claude Levi-**Strauss** (1908–2009) was a Belgian anthropologist and leading structuralist thinker known for his work on kinship, ritual and myth, whose four-volume work *Mythologiques*, exploring codes of expression in different cultures, appeared between 1964 and 1972. His name may conjure up the jeans manufacturer Levi Strauss & Co., although, of course, he has no connection with it whatsoever.

A4

They used quotations from the movie *Casablanca* for the titles of their own works. There's more than one possible answer to the 'odd one out' part.

Play It Again, Sam (1972) stars Woody Allen as a man obsessed with Humphrey Bogart and *Casablanca* in particular. Clips from the film crop up throughout, cleverly giving the impression that Bogart is in dialogue with the cast. Unusually, it wasn't directed by Woody Allen himself but by Herbert Ross – but it's so much a Woody Allen picture that it would be misleading not to name him in the question. This *could* be the odd one out because the title is a (deliberate) *mis*quotation of Ingrid Bergman's line to Dooley Wilson, 'Play it, Sam. Play "As Time Goes By".'

The Usual Suspects, the 1995 noir thriller directed by Bryan Singer, starred Kevin Spacey, Pete Postlethwaite, Gabriel Byrne and Stephen Baldwin. Christopher McQuarrie's screenplay won an Oscar. It's famous for its exceptionally complex plot and the twist at the end which reveals that much of what we've been watching has been a fabrication. Its title also comes from *Casablanca* – Claude Rains's line 'Round up the usual suspects' being the final line of the movie.

We'll Always Have Paris is a late collection (2009) of previously unpublished stories and sketches by Ray Bradbury, the great American writer who died in 2012. He is often described as a science-fiction writer but he protested that his only book in that genre was *Fahrenheit 451*. His short stories, of which he published some 600 during his lifetime, constitute a remarkable body of work. This could also be the odd one out, being a book title rather than a movie.

Q5

Please hum the following: a Slavonic affirmative, an animated Great Dane's second name, a request for new candidates and the first scientologist.

CLUES

- Together they make a phrase which you should be able to hum.
- If you can think of more than one animated Great Dane, you're doing better than us ...

Q6

A jester at an English court began a sequence that went on to include a novel chronicler of women's suffrage, and the woman responsible for the meeting of Anne and Oscar. Who were they? And which French existentialist could be said to have completed the cycle?

CLUES

- For strict accuracy we should pronounce 'Anne' in the Dutch way, as two syllables.
- This could be described as a perennial sequence.

A5

The elements give you Da-doo-ron-ron – so you'd hum the Crystals' 1963 hit song.

A Slavonic affirmative is **Da** (yes).

The best known (only!?) animated Great Dane would be Scooby **Doo**, scrape-prone companion of the gang of the Mystery Machine in the Hanna-Barbera cartoons, whose second name, you could (just about) argue, is **Doo**.

A request for new candidates is **R.O.N.** – an option on a ballot paper standing for Re-Open Nominations, which indicates that the voter rejects all of the named candidates.

The first scientologist is the science-fiction writer and founder of the Church of Scientology – L. **Ron** Hubbard (1911–86)

'Da Doo Ron Ron' was the eighth single by New York girl-group the Crystals, their second UK hit (their fifth in the US), written by crack hit-making team Phil Spector, Ellie Greenwich and Jeff Barry, recorded in March 1963.

A6

It's about the four seasons.

The court jester is Henry VIII's jester Will **Sommers**, said to be the only person at court who could get away with telling the famously volatile king the truth. He survived Henry and remained at court under Queen Mary; he is thought to have died in 1560.

The novelist Howard **Spring** wrote *Fame is the Spur* (1940), the story of the rise of socialism in Britain and the battle for women's suffrage.

The woman who could be said to have arranged a meeting between Anne and Oscar is the actress Shelley **Winters** (1920–2006), who won an Oscar for her role as Mrs van Daan in the 1959 film version of *The Diary of Anne Frank*.

And to complete the cycle, the existentialist writer Albert Camus wrote a novel (published in 1956) called *La Chute* – translated into English, naturally enough, as ***The Fall***.

Q7

Why could you be forgiven for feeling a little claustrophobic in the company of these people?

CLUES

- The man with the telephones is a musician.
- It's the character, not the actor, we need from the second picture.

Q8

Potassium, nickel and iron are sharp; combining sulphur, gold and sodium produces steam; while dogs are happy with tungsten and silver. Can you explain?

CLUES

- The answers are *not* to do with compounds or alloys of these elements, as such.
- In RBQ, as in crosswords, mention of a chemical element often calls simply for its symbol.

A7

Because their names all suggest places where you would keep an animal cooped up.

The first picture is Sir William **Penn**, English Quaker writer and nobleman, the next-door neighbour of Samuel Pepys (popping up frequently in Pepys's diary), and the founder of the state of Pennsylvania.

David Soul played Detective Ken Hutchinson – **'Hutch'** – in the 1970s hit TV series *Starsky and Hutch*.

The man with the telephones is the American modernist composer John **Cage**, pictured installing them for a performance of his work *Variations VII* in 1966. His most notorious work is '4'33"', whose score calls for the musicians to play no notes at all for 4 minutes and 33 seconds, meaning that the work sounds entirely different every time depending on the ambient noise wherever it is being performed.

A8

This is about everyday words made up of chemical symbols.

K (potassium), **Ni** (nickel) and **Fe** (iron) make a sharp **KNiFe; S** (sulphur) **Au** (gold) and **Na** (sodium) produce steam as a **SAuNa; W** (tungsten) and **Ag** (silver) make **WAg**, the action that dogs perform with their tails when they are happy.

All, it will be noted, depend mostly or entirely on those symbols that bear no relation to the English names of the elements. Nearly all of these reflect the elements' Latin names: K for potassium derives from '*kalium*'; Fe for iron from '*ferrum*'; Au for gold from '*aurum*'; Na for sodium from '*natrium*' (our word is a backformed false Latinate derived from 'soda'); and Ag for silver from the Latin '*argentum*' (minus the 'r', to avoid confusion with argon).

The odd one out is W for tungsten, which derives from the name of its main ore, wolframite, known to science long before the element itself was identified. The origin of the name is the German phrase *wolfrahm*, meaning 'wolf's cream'.

Q9

Why might Shearsmith and Pemberton issue an invitation to Bobby Charlton and an unidentified man on the fourth side of 'The White Album'?

CLUES

- 'The White Album' is a reference to the Beatles.
- If you need a further clue, note where this question comes in this quiz.

Q10

Who might be the canine companion of the apostate emperor, the original dreamer of electric sheep, Mrs Morley and the world's first trans MP?

CLUES

- You often find canine companions in children's fiction.
- You may not have heard of all of these people but getting even one or two should give it to you.

A9

Because Reece Shearsmith and Steve Pemberton are the creators of the macabre BBC TV series *Inside No.9* (first broadcast in 2014), and they might therefore invite number-nine-related guests.

Sir Bobby Charlton was arguably the most famous footballer to wear the England **no. 9** shirt, having done so in the World Cups of 1966 and 1970;

The track 'Revolution 9', which takes up a large chunk of the last side of the Beatles' *The Beatles*, known as 'The White Album' (1968), is a heavily experimental eight-minute-plus collage of cut-up sounds and tape loops assembled largely by John Lennon. It includes the repeated phrase **'Number 9'** intoned by a well-spoken English voice. It was sourced from tapes used in Royal Academy of Music examinations, which were stored in the sound library at Abbey Road studios. The writer Ian Macdonald has described 'Revolution 9' as 'the world's most widely distributed avant-garde artefact'.

A10

The four elements in the question give us Julian, Dick, Anne and Georgina – so they represent Enid Blyton's Famous Five, whose canine companion was Timmy the dog.

The Emperor **Julian** (Flavius Claudius Julianus), who ruled Rome from AD 361 to 363, is known as The Apostate because of his reversion from Christianity to paganism.

Do Androids Dream of Electric Sheep? was the novel that inspired the film *Blade Runner*, and is one of the many works of the American science fiction writer Philip K. **Dick**.

'Mrs Morley' was the name Queen **Anne** of England used in her private correspondence with her favourite courtier, Sarah Churchill, Duchess of Marlborough. The Duchess in turn was 'Mrs Freeman'. The nicknames are referred to in the dialogue of the 2018 Oscar-winning movie *The Favourite*, which (very) freely interprets the private life of Queen Anne.

New Zealand politician **Georgina** Beyer, born George Bertrand in 1957, was elected Member for Wairarapa in 1999 and is thought to have been the first transsexual person elected to parliament anywhere in the world. Appropriately and famously, in the Blyton stories cousin Georgina also rebels against her birth gender and insists on being known as George.

ROUND 17

Q1

What law might unite a film about teenage rebellion, a comic-strip character played by Johnny Weissmuller and a lesbian cult novel by Rita Mae Brown?

CLUES

- The film dates from the heyday of teenage rebellion, the 1950s.
- Johnny Weissmuller played Tarzan, but we're looking for a different character here.

Q2

If you connect a song by Hector Berlioz with a medieval allegorical poem and a medieval murder mystery, why are you proving the truth of something Ethel Merman sang?

CLUES

- The murder mystery is medieval in setting, but not in date of composition.
- The role Ethel Merman played could also be relevant to the question.

A1

The law of the jungle.

The film ***The Blackboard Jungle*** (1955), written and directed by Richard Brooks from the novel by Evan Hunter, concerns a young teacher intimidated by his unruly pupils. It appeared at the height of societal fears about the new post-war phenomenon of teenage delinquency. It features a brilliant performance by Sidney Poitier as one of the youths, though he was actually 31 when he made the film.

The comic-strip hero is **Jungle Jim**, created by Alex Raymond in the 1930s, which spawned a series of film adventures (1948–55) with Weissmuller in the title role. An idea of the wide range of his acting talents is conveyed by the contemporary comment that his character was 'Tarzan with clothes on'.

Rubyfruit Jungle (1973) is a novel by Rita Mae Brown with a streetwise lesbian heroine, now regarded as a pioneering example of the frank lesbian coming-of-age story, a genre far more prevalent now than it was at the time. Brown has more recently written a long series of mystery stories 'co-authored' with Sneaky Pie Brown, her cat.

A2

All the clues might prove that – as Ethel Merman sang in the role of Rose in the Sondheim musical *Gypsy* – 'Everything's Coming Up Roses'.

The song by Berlioz is **'La Spectre de la Rose'**, from the cycle *Nuits d'Été* (Summer Nights), Op.7 (1841 for solo voice and piano, then fully orchestrated 1843–56), based on poems by Théophile Gautier.

The medieval poem is the thirteenth-century ***Roman de la Rose*** or *Romance of the Rose*, composed in two sections almost 50 years apart and totalling well over 20,000 lines, which provided source material for Chaucer and other English poets.

The medieval murder mystery – medieval in setting but not in date of authorship – is ***The Name of the Rose*** by Umberto Eco (1980), filmed in 1986 with Sean Connery as the Franciscan friar William of Baskerville investigating mysterious deaths in a monastery in northern Italy in 1327.

Q3

Why might the most famous inhabitant of Bedloe's Island extend a special welcome to visitors wearing red felt caps – and sporting undergarments produced by Messrs Symington?

CLUES

- In theory at least, the inhabitant of Bedloe's Island is there to welcome everybody.
- The undergarments are obsolete, many would say thankfully.

Q4

How could pairing Adam Krug and Morse's creator produce the autobiography of Osbert Sitwell?

CLUES

- Adam Krug is a fictional character, created in the 1940s.
- We've got to hand it to you, if you work this out you'll have done well.

A3

Because the most famous inhabitant of what used to be called Bedloe's Island – in New York Harbour – is the Statue of Liberty (properly titled *Liberty Enlightening the World*), by Frédéric-Auguste Bartholdi, unveiled in 1886. Bedloe's Island was renamed Liberty Island in 1956. As a symbol of liberty she therefore welcomes the free.

The **cap of liberty** was a red felt cap given to freedmen by the Romans, and adapted as a symbol of republican freedom in the French Revolution.

The **liberty bodice** was introduced in the late nineteenth century and produced by R. & W. H. Symington of Market Harborough until the 1960s, by which time it had been worn by many generations of women and girls. Although constraining to modern eyes, it was originally regarded as a huge, liberating advance on the uncomfortable and restricting bones and tight laces of the traditional corset.

A4

They give us the words sinister and dexter, which respectively mean left and right in Latin. The first volume of the aristocratic English writer Sir Osbert Sitwell's autobiography, published in 1945, was entitled *Left Hand, Right Hand* – and this became the overall title of the five-volume series as the remaining books appeared over the next five years.

Adam Krug is the protagonist of the satirical, cryptic ***Bend Sinister*** (1947), the first novel Vladimir Nabokov (1899–1977) wrote after settling in the US. According to Nabokov, the title (a heraldic term meaning a diagonal bar drawn on a shield from upper left from lower right, as opposed to the more normal opposite) suggests a wrong turn taken in life. In the novel this refers to an error of judgement by Krug, a philosopher in a totalitarian state, which results in the death of his young son.

Inspector Morse's creator in a series of novels beginning with *Last Bus to Woodstock* (1975) is **Colin Dexter** (1930–2017).

Q5

What might intoxicate you about a village on the Jurassic coast, a gathering of Morris dancers and a hospital orderly?

CLUES

- *Round Britain Quiz* enthusiasts do tend to have a thirst for knowledge.
- Don't get sidetracked by Lyme (Regis) – that's not the village we're after.

Q6

What prize was achieved by a famously destructive hurricane, a cocktail and an expression of a global fraternal bond, but which very much eluded Castor and Pollux?

CLUES

- They achieved the prize at different times, not all together.
- The theme of this question is musical, and frivolous.

A5

Alcohol.

The village, in East Devon on the Jurassic coast (now a World Heritage Site, known for the copious and important fossil discoveries in the local cliffs) is **Beer**.

The peculiarly English folk tradition of Morris dancing (thought to derive from the term Moorish dancing, suggesting an origin in Spain or north Africa, though the roots are hard to trace) was first recorded in the fifteenth century but enjoyed a revival from the beginning of the twentieth century. An **ale** is a party or gathering of Morris teams at which dances are performed.

A term for a hospital orderly – also used for staff who provide assistance in places such as railway stations, docks and university colleges – is a **porter**.

Beer, ale and porter are all potentially intoxicating.

A6

Despite the promising reference to Classical myth, this is about the Eurovision Song Contest – and some of the UK's successes and failures therein.

The hurricane would be **Katrina** which laid waste to the city of New Orleans, and other areas on the US Gulf Coast, in 2005. Katrina Leskanich, with her band the Waves, won the contest for the UK in 1997 with 'Love Shine a Light'.

The cocktail is a **Bucks Fizz**, which is champagne and orange juice – their perky skirt-ripping routine (and the song 'Making Your Mind Up') won them the contest in 1981.

A global fraternal bond might be one way of describing the **Brotherhood of Man**, whose 'Save Your Kisses for Me' won in 1976 and became that year's bestselling song.

At the other end of the spectrum are the UK's least successful entrants, the Liverpool duo **Jemini**, whose 'Cry Baby' came last in 2003 and suffered the ultimate ignominy of scoring 'nul points'. Subsequently the UK became accustomed, one might say inured, to finishing close to the foot of the table every year. In mythology Castor and Pollux (Polydeuces) are the twin sons of Leda, who was ravished by Zeus in the form of a swan. On their death they were transformed into the twin stars of the constellation Gemini.

Q7

What would have caused Aretha to praise a Jamaican-born singer and model who went Nightclubbing, an American-born actress who became royalty and three British-born cricketers?

CLUES

- The cricketers are brothers.
- The actress *literally* became royalty – not just in a film role.

Q8

Why might the curative invention of a physician, a cat's tongue, the monarchs of Spain and Luxembourg, and a unifying Italian general make your mouth water?

CLUES

- Nibble away at this question one phrase at a time.
- By now we've probably given it to you on a plate.

A7

The fact that they are all named Grace, either as a given name or surname. The late Aretha Franklin's biggest selling album was the gospel recording *Amazing Grace* (1972). A documentary film about the making of the album was unreleased until after her death but became a worldwide success in 2019.

Grace Jones (b.1948), Jamaica-born supermodel, actress and singer, was a well-known figure on the New York nightclub scene long before she recorded the acclaimed album *Nightclubbing* in 1981. It includes some of her best known tracks including 'Demolition Man' and the risqué 'Pull Up to the Bumper'.

Grace Kelly (1929–82) was the Philadelphia-born actress who made her movie debut in *High Noon* in 1952 and went on to star in *Mogambo, The Country Girl* and three films for Alfred Hitchcock: *Dial M for Murder, Rear Window* and *To Catch a Thief.* She married Prince Rainier of Monaco in 1956 and left her Hollywood career behind; she died tragically following a car accident in Monaco in 1982.

The cricketing brothers are the **Grace Brothers**: E. M. Grace, W. G. Grace and Fred Grace, all born in what was then the small village of Downend near Bristol. All three played for the same England Test team in 1880 (Fred tragically died of pneumonia just a few days later). W. G.'s career was the most illustrious of the three: it is hard to think of a more feted British cricketer, ever.

A8

Because they are all types of biscuit.

The physician William Oliver invented the biscuit known as the **Bath Oliver** in about 1750; it's a dry, plain cracker often taken with cheese or port, and was designed to aid the digestion of wealthy visitors to the fashionable spa at Bath trying to make amends for a lifestyle of over-indulgence.

A cat's tongue or a ***langue de chat*** is a small, delicate, buttery biscuit named for its vague resemblance to the shape of a tongue.

The **Bourbon** royal dynasty goes back to late thirteenth-century France; the dynasty held sway in many European territories across the centuries, and Spain and Luxembourg are still ruled by members of the House of Bourbon. The Bourbon chocolate biscuit was given that name in 1930 (after being marketed under the name Creola for 20 years previously).

The Italian general, who played a major role in the unification of Italy in the nineteenth century, was Giuseppe **Garibaldi**. The Garibaldi biscuit was named in his honour, a few years after his visit to Britain, which caused great excitement in 1854.

Q9

A musician whose tune took a veteran soldier to the top of the charts; a Geordie actress who played Queen Bess; and a turn-of-the-century Jewish cuckold with connections in the media, might all be found in the place where the First Fleet landed in Australia. How so?

CLUES

- This is a sweet-smelling question.
- The Geordie actress's achievements go back to pre-Second World War days.

Q10

The similarity between a cross-dressing French diplomat and the James Bond films is as old as time itself. What is it?

CLUES

- The French diplomat is a real-life figure, but from a very long time ago.
- Try not to spend an eternity working this one out.

A9

Because their names are all plant-related; and the place where the 'First Fleet' carrying Australia's first consignment of convicts landed, on 20 January 1788, was Botany Bay. (They didn't actually settle there but moved on, a few miles north, to land six days later at Port Jackson in what's now Sydney Harbour.)

Herbie Flowers (b.1938), composer, trumpeter and bass guitarist, has appeared with David Bowie, Elton John, Lou Reed, Cat Stevens and Paul McCartney. In the late 1970s, along with the guitarist John Williams, he was a member of the virtuoso group Sky, who specialized in rocked-up versions of classical melodies. But his biggest success as a songwriter is the novelty song 'Grandad', a no. 1 hit for Clive Dunn (aka Corporal Jones in *Dad's Army*) in 1970.

Flora Robson (1902–84), the South Shields-born actress, played Elizabeth I in *Fire Over England* (1931) as well as many other tragic and romantic heroines including Zola's Thérèse Raquin in *Guilty* (1944). She was made a Dame of the British Empire in 1960.

Leopold Bloom is the Everyman-hero of James Joyce's *Ulysses* (1922), the Jewish advertisement canvasser for a Dublin newspaper, whose wife Molly commits adultery with another man ('Blazes' Boylan) in Bloom's absence during the single day in 1904 on which the book's action takes place.

A10

Eon.

The eighteenth-century French soldier and diplomat the **Chevalier d'Éon** was noted for an androgynous appearance and an aptitude for passing himself off as a woman, which allowed him to undertake numerous spying activities without being suspected. From the age of 49 onwards he identified as female and dressed consistently as a woman. 'Eonism' became, at one time, a term for transvestism.

The film production company formed by Albert R. Broccoli and Harry Saltzman which has, since 1962, produced the official James Bond film series, is **Eon** Productions. Eon is said to be an acronym for 'everything or nothing'.

An **eon** (or aeon) is a word often used non-specifically or poetically to mean 'since the dawn of time' or 'an impossibly long time'. In astronomy and geology it has more recently been used specifically to mean 10^9 (i.e. 1,000,000,000) years.

ROUND 18

Q1

Can you put these people into chronological order?

CLUES

- Forget about their actual birth dates.
- You might reasonably describe them all as showbusiness royalty.

Q2

Madiba might share common beginnings with a defunct checkpoint in Jerusalem, a computer pattern relating to chaos theory and a British master of spin. Who or what are they all?

CLUES

- Madiba is a nickname for a very eminent world leader of recent history.
- 'Master of spin' is not a reference to a cricketer.

A1

Each of the stars' surnames is also the name of one of the royal houses of England, so it is those whose chronological order we're after.

They are Rod **Stewart** (i.e. Stuart), b. 1945; the operatic soprano Jessye **Norman**, born in Augusta, Georgia, in 1945; and Dame Barbara **Windsor**, née Deeks, b.1937, sex symbol of the *Carry On* movies in the 1960s and 1970s, latterly a key member of the cast of *EastEnders* as the formidable matriarch and landlady Peggy Mitchell.

So the correct order is Norman (1066–1154), Stuart (1603–1714), Windsor (1917–), 17 July 1917 being the date when George V promulgated the change of name from Saxe-Coburg-Gotha to Windsor.

Somebody who knows their Scottish history, however, might give a slightly different, and better-informed, answer, to the effect that the Stewarts were the ruling family of Scotland before the Stuarts took over in England (having changed the spelling of their name), from the accession of Robert II in 1371 to James VI's move to London in 1603. Stewart is, in any case, the etymologically correct spelling, reflecting the family's descent from Walter the Steward.

A2

These are all names beginning with the letters Mandel – thus their 'common beginnings'.

Madiba is the Xhosa name now often applied reverentially to the Nobel Peace Prize-winning South African head of state Nelson **Mandela** (1918–2013).

The checkpoint is the **Mandelbaum** Gate, which between 1948 and 1967 was the crossing-point between the Israeli and Jordanian halves of divided Jerusalem.

A computer-generated, infinitely repeating pattern, which relates to the conditions in which chaos theory operates, is known as a **Mandelbrot** set.

The political figure, architect of the New Labour project in the 1990s and one of the earliest figures in the UK to earn the title of 'spin doctor' (as well as the sobriquet 'the Prince of Darkness' among his enemies) is Peter **Mandelson**, Baron Mandelson (b.1953). His maternal grandfather was the leading 1940s Labour politician and cabinet minister Herbert Morrison.

Q3

Washington – Washington – Buffalo – Dallas. What's the significance of this sequence?

CLUES

- These are the only four in this sequence to date.
- It's not a sporting sequence.

Q4

An ancient stone, who has several daughters, is certainly the oldest; another was a notorious London character in Tudor times; and a third went back to Edinburgh Castle in the nineteenth century, though she dates from long before that. Who are they?

CLUES

- They are all referred to as female, though in fact two of them are inanimate objects.
- The ancient stone is in the far north of England.

A3

These are the locations, in chronological order, of the assassinations of the four US presidents who have been killed in office.

Abraham Lincoln was shot by John Wilkes Booth at Ford's Theatre in Washington, DC in 1865.

James Garfield was shot by Charles J. Guiteau at the Baltimore & Potomac Railroad Station in Washington in 1881 – he died 79 days later of sepsis and pneumonia resulting from his wounds.

William McKinley was shot by the reclusive Polish-American anarchist Leon Czolgosz as he visited the Pan-American Exposition in Buffalo, NY, in September 1901.

And, of course, **John F. Kennedy** was shot by Lee Harvey Oswald in Dealey Plaza in Dallas in November 1963.

A4

Megs.

'Long Meg and her daughters', the third-largest stone circle in Britain, are prehistoric standing stones at Little Salkeld near Penrith in Cumbria. Meg is a 15-foot sandstone pillar, and her daughters are smaller boulders, 69 or so in number. Local legend has it that every time you count them, you get a different number. If you count them twice and the number is the same, they will come to life as witches. The stones are the subject of a sonnet by Wordsworth from about 1821 and a terrific poem by Andrew Young, 1936.

Long Meg of Westminster was a legendary figure dating from the London of the reign of Henry VIII. Little is known about her for certain, but she may have been an innkeeper or brothel-keeper; she became notorious for her fiery character and outrageous exploits, celebrated and embellished in ballads and chap-books for many years after her death.

Mons Meg is a huge fifteenth-century cannon made at Mons in what is now Belgium and given to James II of Scotland, who used it in 1455 against the Douglases at Threave Castle. It was used in further sieges until the sixteenth century and kept at Edinburgh Castle until 1754 when it was taken to the Tower of London. It was returned to Edinburgh in 1829 at Sir Walter Scott's request. (It has nothing to do with the First World War Battle of Mons.)

Q5

Why might an art gallery in Liverpool, a colourful housing development in Newcastle, an avuncular popularizer of horticulture and a friend to the Flytes all display a competitive streak?

CLUES

- A bit of teamwork could come in handy here.
- The popularizer of horticulture is no longer with us, but was known at one time by more or less the whole British nation.

Q6

Why are a royal mountain, some muddy water, a trading point and two queens, one of them specific, among the greatest glories of a settlement that stretches from sea to sea?

CLUES

- The word 'settlement' is used for a reason, though it is deliberately misleading.
- The specific queen is Victoria.

A5

Their names all suggest athletic competition and they might therefore all be encountered at an athletics tournament or the Olympic Games.

The **Walker** Art Gallery, a Liverpool landmark and home to one of the UK's most important art collections, opened in 1877.

The colourful and award-winning **Byker** Wall development was designed by Ralph Erskine to replace cleared slums in the east end of Newcastle in the 1970s.

The popularizer of horticulture is Percy **Thrower** (1913–88), gardener, writer and broadcaster, loved by generations of TV viewers in the UK for his gentle presentation style.

The protagonist of *Brideshead Revisited*, Evelyn Waugh's novel published in 1945, is Charles **Ryder**. He befriends the wealthy Flyte family after becoming close to the wayward Sebastian as a student at Oxford. In the famous TV adaptation of the 1980s he was portrayed by Jeremy Irons.

A6

The 'settlement' is Canada, whose name derives from an Iroquoian word for a settlement, and whose national motto is *a mari usque ad mari* ('from sea to sea') – and these are references to five of its major cities.

The royal mountain is **Montreal** (Quebec), named for the hill in the centre of the city. **Winnipeg** (Manitoba) means the place of muddy water, a Western Cree name first applied to Lake Winnipeg. The capital city **Ottawa** takes its name from an Algonquin word meaning trade, first applied to the River Ottawa on which it stands. **Regina** (Saskatchewan) is Latin for a queen, and **Victoria** (British Columbia) is the specific queen.

Q7

What connects a pair of atmospheric radiation bands, a towering art-deco masterpiece, and a court procedure offering resolution when it's six of one and half-a-dozen of the other?

CLUES

- You will be misled by 'court procedure' if you assume it's to do with the law.
- If we said 'belts' instead of 'bands', that might help you.

Q8

How do you know you can count on Danny's gang, Lumet's jurors and Thurber's clocks?

CLUES

- In RBQ-land, the expression 'to count on' is usually a signal that numbers are involved.
- Danny's gang is a criminal gang.

A7

This is about the achievements of three people called Van Allen or Van Alen.

The Van Allen Belts of charged particles around the Earth were described by the American physicist **James Van Allen** (1914–2006). He became interested in the detection of cosmic rays and helped to develop the USA's first satellite, Explorer I, in 1958, with his cosmic ray detector aboard. Satellite observations showed that the Earth's magnetic field traps high speed charged particles in two belt-shaped zones.

New York's art-deco Chrysler Building, completed in 1929, was the work of the architect **William Van Alen** (1883–1954). Walter Chrysler simply told Van Alen: 'Make it higher than the Eiffel Tower.' He did: it measured 1,046 feet including the surmounting spire; but its supremacy as the world's tallest structure only lasted a couple of years, until the completion of the Empire State Building in 1931.

'Court procedure' is an allusion to the tennis tie-breaker, devised by **James Van Alen** (1902–91), which comes into play when the score in a set stands at six games all. Van Alen was also the founder of the International Tennis Hall of Fame, the world's largest tennis museum, at Newport, Rhode Island.

A8

This is a numerical sequence.

Danny (Ocean)'s gang in the 1960 film starring Frank Sinatra, Peter Lawford, Dean Martin, Joey Bishop and Sammy Davis Jr, and in the Steven Soderbergh remake of 2001, is ***Ocean's Eleven***.

Sidney Lumet directed Henry Fonda and 11 others in the claustrophobic courtroom classic ***Twelve Angry Men*** (1957).

James Thurber wrote the fantasy story ***The Thirteen Clocks*** (1950).

Q9

Where you would go to earn your crust; what you would use to keep you dry on the way; what you would ask someone who claimed to recognize you; what you would call him if he insulted you; what you would do if everyone applauded; and what you might wear if you made a huge success of all of this. Who might you be, if all of this applied to you?

CLUES

- Take one of these phrases and give the first answer that comes into your head: you may see the theme quickly.
- You might be someone known only by their first name.

Q10

Why might the author of *The Periodic Table*, an anti-apartheid campaigner and Pam Ewing all deserve priority treatment?

CLUES

- *The Periodic Table* is a creative work, which is why it's italicized: we don't mean the compiler of the periodic table of elements.
- The anti-apartheid campaigner is a woman.

A9

You might be Rihanna – because these phrases all suggest titles of some of her hit songs between 2007 and 2016.

To earn your crust you would go to **'Work'**; to stay dry you would use an **'Umbrella'**; if someone claimed to recognize you, you might ask **'What's My Name?'**, and if they insulted you, you would call them a **'Rude Boy'**. After being applauded you would **'Take a Bow'** and if you made a huge success of it all you would wear **'Diamonds'**.

A10

Because they have names which imply that they are 'number one'.

Primo Levi (1919–87) was the author of *The Periodic Table*, not a chemistry textbook (though Levi was a chemist) but a collection of autobiographical short stories that amount to a restrained and moving account of survival in the Nazi concentration camps.

Ruth First (1925–82) was an early member of the African National Congress. In 1949 she married lawyer and labour organizer Joe Slovo, another white member of the ANC; both were tried and acquitted at the Treason Trial of 1956. Their friends included leaders such as Walter Sisulu and Nelson Mandela. In 1982 she was assassinated while living in exile.

Victoria Principal (b.1950) played Pamela Ewing in *Dallas*. A central character through the show's entire run, Pam was the wife of J. R. Ewing's younger brother Bobby (Patrick Duffy) and sister of rival oil tycoon Cliff Barnes (Ken Kercheval).

ROUND 19

Q1

In what kind of landscape might you encounter a veteran *Spectator* cartoonist, one who was sculpted in solid gold and the inventor of a reliable test for arsenic?

CLUES

- The solid gold sculpture is real, not fictional or mythological.
- Hopefully this one won't be too much of an uphill struggle.

Q2

What Formula might Brazilians apply to a great Flemish painter, the author of *Self-Reliance* and the First Duke of Bronté?

CLUES

- The First Duke of Bronté is much better known by another title: he is a hero in British history.
- If you get the surnames of these people, you then have to think of them as first names.

A1

On the moors, or somewhere similar: their names are Heath, Moss and Marsh, all names used for a boggy expanse of upland.

The veteran cartoonist is Michael **Heath** (b.1935), since 1991 cartoon editor of the *Spectator* and creator of memorable series such as *Private Eye*'s *The Regulars* and *Great Bores of Today*. His characters have often drawn inspiration from the Soho social scene he was part of in the 1960s, alongside Jeffrey Bernard, Lucian Freud and Francis Bacon.

Someone sculpted in gold is the British supermodel Kate **Moss** (b.1974), subject of the work by Marc Quinn entitled *Siren* exhibited at the British Museum in 2008. It depicts a lifesize Kate Moss with her legs wrapped behind her head, and is made of solid 18-carat gold, promoted at the time as 'the largest pure gold sculpture since ancient Egypt'.

The **Marsh** test was developed by the British chemist James Marsh (1794–1846) for detecting tiny traces of arsenic, a popular choice of substance for poisoners in Victorian times. It was widely adopted by the newly established police force and was a significant development in the history of forensic science.

A2

The capital F suggests Formula One, and this celebrates three Brazilian racing drivers. In each case, the surname suggested in the question gives us the Christian name of the driver.

So the painter Pieter Paul **Rubens** (1577–1640) gives us **Rubens Barrichello** (b.1972).

Self-Reliance was a work by the American writer Ralph Waldo **Emerson** (1803–82) in which he expounds his belief that one should avoid conformity and a slavish unthinking adherence to commonly held notions, and instead be true to one's own instincts and ideas. As Emerson himself put it, in what is probably the most famous line from the essay: 'A foolish consistency is the hobgoblin of little minds'. His surname gives us **Emerson Fittipaldi**, (b.1946; World Champion 1972 and 1974).

The Duke of Bronté was not a relative of the literary sisters of Haworth but a title conferred on Horatio **Nelson** by the King of Naples after Nelson had restored him to his throne in 1799. **Nelson Piquet** (b.1952) won the Formula One World Championship in 1981, 1983 and 1987, having changed his name from Nelson Souto Maior to stop his parents finding out about his motor-racing career.

Q3

For your starter, choose a Nicaraguan presidential dynasty; you'll have whetted your appetite for the mistress of a prime minister, and a lyricist who is far from EGOT-istical; and you can wash it all down with a dog. What kind of restaurant are you in?

CLUES

- The mistress of a prime minister is in recent history (so it's not Lloyd George's mistress, for example).
- You'll need to make sure the water jug is topped up.

Q4

Why might you find Lucifer, Kingsley Amis's Colonel and Francisco Salva's most important invention right on your doorstep?

CLUES

- You won't have heard of Francisco Salva but you will have heard of his invention, and heard a lot *as a result* of his invention.
- Confusingly, thinking of books by Kingsley Amis may not help much.

A3

You're in an Indian restaurant.

The Nicaraguan dictator, President Anastasio **Somoza** (b.1896, assassinated 1956), was succeeded by his sons Luis Somoza Debayle (1922–67) and Anastasio Somoza Debayle (1925–80). A samosa (difference in pronunciation negligible) is a spicy pastry pyramid filled with meat and/or vegetables.

The prime minister's mistress is Edwina **Currie** (b.1946), whose four-year affair with John Major while he was a rising cabinet star was sensationally revealed with the publication of her diaries in 2002. She was the Conservative MP for Derbyshire South, a junior minister in the Department of Health and a prominent media performer.

Sir Tim **Rice** (b.1944), the lyricist of the hugely successful musicals *Jesus Christ Superstar, Evita, Chess, The Lion King* and *Aladdin* among others, is one of the very few people to have won an Emmy, a Grammy, an Oscar and a Tony Award during their career – a grand slam known, for obvious reasons, as EGOT. Despite this, he remains self-effacing.

To accompany this tasty meal you might order a jug of **Lassi(e)** – a sweet yoghurt drink.

A4

Because the clues lead to the titles of three major British newspapers, which might (even in our online age) drop onto the doormat in the morning, namely the *Morning Star*, the *Sun* and the *Telegraph*.

The word 'Lucifer' literally means 'light-bearer', and, as well as referring to the fallen angel of *Paradise Lost*, is the Roman astrological term for the planet Venus in its guise as the **morning star**, a translation of the Greek term '*eosphoros*' or 'phosphorus', which has the more specific meaning of 'dawn-bearer'

Kingsley Amis wrote a James Bond novel in 1968 entitled *Colonel* ***Sun***, intended as a sequel and homage to the Ian Fleming books he admired. It appeared under the pseudonym Robert Markham – but the author's real identity became well known.

The **telegraph** was the cumulative product of work by several inventors, but the earliest working prototype, which predated the development of the voltaic cell, was the electrostatic telegraph produced by the Spanish physicist Francisco Salva (1751–1828). Other inventors with a legitimate claim to the device's creation include Samuel von Sömmering, Paul Schilling, Carl Friedrich Gauss, Wilhelm Weber and Sir William Fothergill Cooke, who patented the first commercial electric telegraph in 1837.

Q5

In which room of the house would you be most likely to find a hit Elvis sang in *Loving You*, Ibsen's drama about Torvald and Nora, and a D. H. Lawrence story filmed in 1949?

CLUES

- It would probably have to be quite an old-fashioned house.
- It's a playful connection.

Q6

If Manchester provided you with a conversation between, say, the Queen and Prince Charles; Sheffield would send Miller potty; and Charles Foster Kane would be in Glasgow – what would drive you to Hull?

CLUES

- Don't make too much of a drama out of this one.
- 'Wolfie' Smith could be in Glasgow too.

A5

The answer is a child's bedroom or nursery.

'(Let Me Be Your) **Teddy Bear**' was sung by Elvis Presley in his second movie, *Loving You*, and reached no. 1 in the US (no. 3 in the UK) as a single in 1957.

Troubled husband and wife Torvald and Nora Helmer are the main characters in the Ibsen play ***A Doll's House*** (1879).

The D. H. Lawrence short story is 'The **Rocking Horse** Winner', the story of a child with an uncanny ability to predict racing winners while riding his rocking horse. It was filmed in 1949 with John Mills and the young John Howard Davies.

A6

A Truck. The link here is British regional theatres.

The conversation between the two members of the royal family gives us Manchester's **Royal Exchange** (founded 1976).

The Sheffield **Crucible** recalls both the Arthur Miller play and the snooker venue; the theatre was opened in 1971 to replace the old Sheffield Playhouse, and takes its name from the crucible process of steel production, pioneered in Sheffield in the 1740s by Benjamin Huntsman.

Charles Foster Kane is *Citizen Kane* in the Orson Welles film and could thus be found at Glasgow **Citizens** Theatre, founded by James Bridie in the 1940s.

That just leaves a drive to Hull **Truck**. Hull Truck Theatre was opened in 1971 by actor Mike Bradwell who placed an advert in *Time Out*: 'Half-formed theatre company seeks other half'. John Godber was appointed creative director in 1984 and his formal association with Hull Truck continued for the next 26 years.

Q7

Why might Jean de Dinteville and Georges de Selve read a late masterpiece by Henry James while being driven in the definitive Indian motor car?

CLUES

- Even if you've never heard of Jean de Dinteville and Georges de Selve you will probably be familiar with what they look like.
- We have to be diplomatic with any clues we give you.

Q8

What could it be about a US prosecuting official, the unified atomic mass unit and a Teddy boy's haircut that would interest the man who documented Bob Dylan's tour of Britain?

CLUES

- The prosecuting official is a reference to a generic title rather than a specific person.
- The Bob Dylan tour was in the 1960s.

A7

They are all Ambassadors.

Jean de Dinteville and Georges de Selve are the two subjects in Hans Holbein's large canvas known as ***The Ambassadors***, finished in 1533, now in the National Gallery.

Henry James's dark comedy ***The Ambassadors*** (1903) is considered one of his finest late novels.

The Hindustan **Ambassador**, based on the 1950s Morris Oxford, was in production from 1958 to 2014 and was the ubiquitous car on Indian roads throughout the late twentieth century.

A8

The director of the film *Dont Look Back* (there is deliberately no apostrophe), chronicling Bob Dylan's 1965 concert tour of the UK, was D. A. Pennebaker – and the others are all D. A.s of one kind or another.

D(onn) A(lan) Pennebaker (b.1925) was approached by manager Albert Grossman to film Dylan's British tour, after his documentary on the jazz musician Dave Lambert came to prominence following Lambert's tragic death in a car crash. The movie *Dont Look Back* contains candid footage of Dylan in performance, backstage and in conversation, and incidentally documents his increasingly obvious break-up with Joan Baez. It includes the famous sequence in which Dylan, standing in an alleyway, holds up cards bearing lyrics from the song 'Subterranean Homesick Blues' and throws them away as the song proceeds.

In the US legal system a District Attorney or **D. A.** is the government-appointed (or elected) official responsible for prosecutions. Among the memorable lyrics in 'Subterranean Homesick Blues', coincidentally, is: 'Maggie says that many say / They must bust in early May / Orders from the D. A.'

The standard scientific unit of atomic mass is the unified atomic mass unit or the dalton, named after the Manchester chemist John Dalton (1766–1844), and abbreviated **Da**.

A hairstyle popular with Teddy boys in 1950s Britain was the **D. A.** or 'duck's arse', where the hair was combed back into a ridge or seam at the back of the head, often held with Brylcreem.

Q9

On what grounds could you expect a Rossini opera to be set in Newcastle, a US news network to be based in Leicester, a wartime thriller to be set in south London, Lewis Carroll's Alice to meet an eccentric character from Luton, and a Chekhov play to be staged in Brighton?

CLUES

- The phrase 'on what grounds', in the context of these cities, is a heavy hint.
- Kick this one around for a while and see where it gets you.

Q10

A shanty town in the Depression, the principle of the free market and a twenty-first-century programme of health insurance are all in the dictionary, but a long way apart – so what do they have in common?

CLUES

- They are likely to be in the *OED* but they will *definitely* be in Webster's.
- Think of journalistic jargon that entered the language.

A9

On *football* grounds: the link is English league football clubs' nicknames.

The Rossini opera is ***The Thieving Magpie*** (*La Gazza Ladra*, 1817) – **Newcastle United** are the **Magpies.** Clearly there is another cheeky Newcastle United connection (if you mispronounce the Italian *Gazza*).

Rupert Murdoch's network in the US is **Fox News** – **Leicester City** are the **Foxes**.

Where Eagles Dare (1968), based on the novel by Alistair MacLean, is a Second World War action film starring Richard Burton and Clint Eastwood – **Crystal Palace** are the **Eagles**.

Alice meets the **Mad Hatter** at the tea party – **Luton Town** are the **Hatters** (so named because Luton was for centuries a centre of hat manufacture, particularly straw hats). The fumes given off by the glue used in hat-making were notoriously supposed to send factory workers mad after inhaling them for years on end, hence the phrase 'mad as a hatter', inspiring Carroll's character.

Finally, a Chekhov play would be ***The Seagull*** (1896) – **Brighton & Hove Albion** are the **Seagulls**.

A10

These are all words, incorporating the names of the US presidents with whom they are associated, that have entered the language.

Hooverville was the name given to any of several thousand shanty towns built to shelter the homeless in the US after the crash of 1929. They were named for Herbert Hoover who was president at the time and on whom the crash was widely blamed.

Reaganomics is the orthodoxy that the best way to run the economy is to allow the greatest reasonable leeway for the free market, famously espoused by President Ronald Reagan in the 1980s.

Obamacare is the system of health insurance introduced in 2010 by Barack Obama, against fierce opposition, which provided health care to some 20 million previously uninsured Americans. His successor made it a pledge of his election campaign to dismantle it.

ROUND 20

Q1

In which famous sequence is a complaint about miserliness followed by Louis XIV, someone unpleasant with a condiment connection, a synthetic beauty, an unorthodox homecoming and blessed repose?

CLUES

- It's a musical sequence.
- Think of four people crossing a road.

Q2

In a sentence can you say: what a revered England goalie does to protect his earnings; how a stellar guitarist's manager responds to a request for his client; and how a Yorkshire announcer preserves his vegetables?

CLUES

- Trademark *Round Britain Quiz* puns are involved here.
- We should really have said, 'In three very short sentences ...'

A1

The long medley of songs on side two of the Beatles' *Abbey Road* album (1969), mainly composed by Paul McCartney.

The titles hinted at in the question are, respectively: **'You Never Give Me Your Money'**, **'Sun King'**, **'Mean Mr Mustard'**, **'Polythene Pam'**, **'She Came In Through the Bathroom Window'** and **'Golden Slumbers'**.

A2

These are people whose names are a sentence in themselves.

What a football goalie does to protect his earnings: **'Gordon Banks'**. Banks (b.1937) kept goal for England's 1966 World Cup-winning side, was awarded the OBE in 1970, and won the Football Writers' Association Player of the Year award in 1972.

How a stellar guitarist's manager responds to a request for his client: **'Brian May'**. May (b.1947), guitarist with Queen since 1972, is still very much involved in the surviving band's projects. He finally completed his long-abandoned PhD thesis, 'A study of radial velocities in the zodiacal dust cloud', in 2007.

How a Yorkshire announcer preserves his vegetables: **'Wilfred Pickles'**. Pickles (1904–78) was the BBC newsreader whose Halifax vowels caused a stir in the 1940s; he became a successful TV presenter and game-show host, routinely with his wife Mabel 'at the table'.

Q3

Can you arrange in order of importance: the husband to whom Tess is finally reconciled, Martin's epic Game, a U-2 pilot, a Russian White Sea port and medieval Wales?

CLUES

- Tess refers to *Tess of the D'Urbervilles* and the epic Game is exactly what you think it is.
- This is a heavenly question.

Q4

Separate and unite; approve and denounce; fasten up and collapse. Why might these pairs appear to prove the similarity of opposites?

CLUES

- We're looking for synonyms for these words.
- The question provides examples of why English may be a tricky language to learn.

A3

These are clues to five of the nine orders of angels in Christian mythology. The nine orders (in descending order) are usually taken to be Seraphim, Cherubim, Thrones, Dominions, Virtues, Powers, Principalities, Archangels and Angels.

The husband who marries Tess in Hardy's *Tess of the D'Urbervilles* (1891) is **Angel** Clare. When she confesses on their wedding night that her virginity was taken against her will by Alec d'Urberville, he abandons her and goes to live in Brazil. Only near the end are they reconciled, before Tess is arrested at Stonehenge, tried and hanged.

The U-2 pilot is Gary **Powers** (1929–77), whose U-2 spy-plane flying a CIA reconnaissance mission was shot down by a Soviet missile in 1960. He was captured and interrogated by the KGB for several months. The incident was a pivotal moment of distrust in the Cold War. He was convicted of espionage and imprisoned in the USSR for two years, until sent home as part of a spy-swap in Berlin in 1962.

George R. R. Martin's epic series of novels *A Song of Ice and Fire* and the TV phenomenon they spawned are known universally as *Game of* ***Thrones***.

The port on the White Sea is **Archangel** or Arkhangelsk, at the mouth of the Dvina River in European Russia, some 700 miles from Moscow. According to legend it was near here that the Archangel Michael slew the devil, and the city's coat of arms bears an image of that happy event.

The **Principality** of Wales, i.e. the land ruled by the Prince of Wales, lasted from 1216 to 1536 and at its height encompassed about two-thirds of the modern territory of Wales. Wales is still sometimes informally referred to as 'the Principality', though it isn't one.

A4

This is about words that have the same meaning as their antonym – sometimes known as a contronym or auto-antonym.

Cleave can be both to separate and unite; **sanction** can mean both approve and denounce; and **buckle** means both to fasten and to collapse.

Q5

Why might Richard Wilson be incredulous at a boys' comic, Dr Frankenstein and the Radio Corporation of America?

CLUES

- He would be incredulous if he was in character.
- You're onto a winner with this one.

Q6

What do these people have in common?

CLUES

- The little girl in the middle picture inspired a famous fictional character.
- The runner inspired a famous film.

A5

He'd probably shout 'I don't believe it!' in the role of Victor Meldrew – because these are all famous Victors.

The boys' comic the ***Victor*** was published by D. C. Thomson of Dundee in 1961–92. Its stock-in-trade was Second World War stories of bravery with lots of colourful explosions, but it also carried strips about football and some more comedic *Beano*-style characters. Regular features included 'Joe Bones the Human Fly', 'The Goals of Jimmy Grant' and 'Into Battle with Matt Braddock'.

Dr Frankenstein's first name in the 1818 novel by Mary Shelley is **Victor**.

The Radio Corporation of America bought the Victor Talking Machine Company in 1929 and became **RCA Victor**. The company 'invented' the 7-inch single, launching the first gramophone disc of this size in 1949. The legend 'RCA Victor' continued to appear on many of the company's records, including those by Elvis Presley, Harry Nilsson, the Kinks, John Denver, Jim Reeves and David Bowie, as late as the 1970s.

A6

They are linked by the surname Liddell, with slight variations in spelling and pronunciation.

The story of the Scottish athlete and missionary **Eric Henry Liddell** (1902–45), pictured here, is told in the film *Chariots of Fire*.

The young photographic model is **Alice Liddell** (1852–1934), of whom Charles Lutwidge Dodgson (Lewis Carroll) made many photographic images, and for whom the *Alice* stories were originally written. She was the daughter of the eminent Classical scholar Henry George Liddell, best known for the Greek-English Lexicon.

Alvar Lidell was a BBC announcer and newsreader, deputy chief announcer from 1937. He famously announced the abdication of Edward VIII; and in 1939 read the ultimatum to Germany from a room at 10 Downing Street, and introduced the prime minister as he broke the news that Britain was at war. He retired in 1969 and died in 1981.

Q7

In what sense does royalty own a chat-show host and a prime minister in Birmingham, the heroine of *Georgy Girl* in Norfolk and the creator of *The Demon Headmaster* in London?

CLUES

- Place names in the UK often contain clues about their history.
- In the case of London there is a railway connection.

Q8

Why might a Leon Garfield villain, the still-familiar product of a royal decree of 1801 and Lord John Russell think they were all right?

CLUES

- They all have a name (or nickname, at least) in common.
- Thinking of Peter Sellers might give you a further leg up.

A7

This is about UK place names that have a royal possessive in them. Strictly speaking, of course, it doesn't mean they are really owned by the Crown to any greater extent than anywhere else.

King's **Norton**, as in Graham, and King's **Heath**, as in Sir Edward, are both in Birmingham (another example of the latter can also be found in Leicestershire); King's **Lynn**, as in the actress Lynn Redgrave (1943–2010), of the celebrated Redgrave acting dynasty, the Oscar-nominated star of the 1966 film *Georgy Girl*; and King's **Cross**, as in the children's writer Gillian Cross, creator of the *Demon Headmaster* series.

A8

Because they are all Jacks, as in the popular phrase usually used as a denouncement of those who look after their own interests – 'I'm all right Jack'. The 1959 Boulting Brothers' film comedy of that title starred Peter Sellers.

Among the works of the children's writer Leon Garfield (1921–96) is ***Black Jack***, a novel set (like many of his stories) in the eighteenth century and featuring the adventures of a boy called Bartholomew Dorking with a murderer who has survived a hanging. It was filmed in 1979 by Ken Loach.

A royal declaration by George III in 1801 following the formal union of Great Britain and Ireland led to the adoption of the Union flag of the United Kingdom, known almost universally as the **Union Jack**. It combines the cross of St George with the saltires of St Andrew and St Patrick. Strictly speaking a Jack is a naval flag worn on the jackstaff in the bows of a warship, but those who insist that the flag should not be called the Union Jack are usually regarded as pedants.

Lord John Russell, the Victorian Whig politician and reformer who was twice prime minister (1846–52 and 1865–66), was nicknamed **Finality Jack**. The nickname arose from his assertion that the great Reform Act of 1832 was a 'finality'. In the event he made several attempts to further reform the parliamentary system and extend the franchise during his political career.

Q9

Transform something sweet into a fake, fertile ground into a story with a moral, and a specific measurement of length into an unspecific measurement of volume – but do it very quietly.

CLUES

- The measurement of length is an imperial measurement.
- The means of transformation is the same in each case.

Q10

What would a Lincoln mathematician who invented a system of logical formulation, a feared recluse in Maycomb and a motorbiking private investigator of the 1980s say to a goose?

CLUES

- The private investigator is a TV character.
- The feared recluse's name was borrowed by a British pop group.

A9

These are three word transformations achieved by adding the initial letter P.

Honey becomes **phoney; arable** becomes a **parable; inch** becomes a **pinch** (as in a pinch of salt).

The additions add up to **ppp**, which is an instruction on a musical score to play very quietly.

A10

The phrase has it that you would (or wouldn't) 'say boo to a goose': and these are three people whose names begin with Boo–.

The Lincoln mathematician is George **Boole** (1815–64) who gave his name to Boolean algebra, a way of describing logical relations using mathematical symbols.

In the novel *To Kill a Mockingbird*, the feared recluse living in the tumbledown old house across the way from where Scout and Jem live, in Maycomb, Alabama, is **Boo** Radley.

The motorbiking private investigator is fireman-turned sleuth Ken **Boon** in the 1980s TV crime series which ran from 1986 to 1995. He was played by Michael Elphick, and his trademark was the red and silver 'White Lightning' motorbike he always rode.

ROUND 21

Q1

If you sent Brucie, along with the authors of *Esio Trot*, *The Virginian* and *The Crossing of Antarctica*, to Iowa, they would all end up in someone's garden. How is this?

CLUES

- *Esio Trot* is a children's book, far from the best known work of its creator.
- Knowing the common abbreviation for Iowa will help you.

Q2

Why might you find yourself chasing a 1930s Wimbledon star, an associate of Bob Marley, a fellow inmate of Fletch and a test cricketer from Tyneside out of your vegetable patch?

CLUES

- This is to do with their nicknames.
- The Wimbledon star is British – but is not Fred Perry.

A1

'Sending someone to' Iowa in this context entails adding the common US postal abbreviation IA to the three names clued in the question. It produces four familiar plants.

The late Sir Bruce Forsyth (1928–2017) thus gives us **forsythia**, a plant closely connected to one of his ancestors, the eighteenth-century botanist and founder member of the Royal Horticultural Society William Forsyth, in whose honour the shrub forsythia was named.

Roald Dahl (1916–90) wrote *Esio Trot*, a sweet tale in which a lonely man wins the heart of his neighbour by convincing her that he can make her pet tortoise double in size, using the magic words 'Esio trot' (which is 'tortoise' backwards). Adding –ia to Dahl's surname gives us a **dahlia**.

The Virginian (1902) was the best-remembered fictional work of Owen Wister (1860–1938), and gave rise to various film and TV versions. James Drury played the title character in the TV Western which ran to nine series, 1962–71. Adding –ia to Wister gives us **wisteria.**

Finally, the explorer Sir Vivian Fuchs (1908–99), together with Sir Edmund Hillary, described in his 1958 book *The Crossing of Antarctica* their successful attempt earlier that year to drive from the Weddell Sea to the Ross Sea, a journey of 2,158 miles lasting 99 days. The same procedure with his name gives us a **fuchsia**. (All of these plants having, of course, actually been named after other people bearing those surnames.)

A2

You'd chase them out of your vegetable patch because they are all nicknamed Bunny.

They are: **Edward 'Bunny' Austin (1906–2000)**, British tennis star, five-times singles finalist at Wimbledon, runner-up in 1932 and 1938; reggae musician **Bunny Wailer** (Neville Livingston, b.1947), original member of the Wailers alongside Bob Marley and Peter Tosh; **'Bunny' Warren**, the affably dense inmate of Slade Prison played by Sam Kelly in the classic BBC TV soap *Porridge* in 1973–7; Graham **'Bunny'** Onions (b.1982), Gateshead-born England test cricketer.

Q3

Which mythical giant might cast an envious eye at Zaphod Beeblebrox, Steve Martin, and Desdemona and Othello – and why?

CLUES

- Desdemona and Othello are relevant to this question as a pair, rather than as individuals.
- An envious eye, in the singular, is significant.

Q4

To get to the Crab nebula, set controls for Leeds. To reach the Trifid nebula, head for the Channel Tunnel. For the Orion nebula, meanwhile, you'd skirt Birmingham to the south and east. Can you explain why?

CLUES

- Think of other ways in which these nebulae might be described or classified.
- Your satnav can't find places that are not on the Earth's surface so you may have to tap in the next best thing.

A3

The Cyclops, Polyphemus – because he had only one eye, where people normally have two – and the others have two of something that you only normally have one of.

Zaphod Beeblebrox, the alien character in Douglas Adams's *Hitch-Hiker's Guide to the Galaxy* radio series (and novels, TV series and film), has **two heads**.

Steve Martin, in one of his funniest films plays *The Man with* ***Two Brains*** (1983, dir. Carl Reiner). Brain surgeon Dr Hfuhruhurr, frustrated by his sexless marriage to Kathleen Turner, falls in love with the preserved brain of a dead woman (voiced by Sissy Spacek). Desperate to consummate his love, he attempts to find a brainless body in which to transplant the beloved brain.

Iago, in the opening scene of *Othello*, rouses Desdemona's father Brabanzio from his bed to tell him: 'I am one, sir, that comes to tell you your daughter and the Moor are now making the beast with **two backs**'. (It's the best-known literary occurrence of the phrase, but it wasn't original to Shakespeare – it had been used by Rabelais 70 years earlier.)

A4

The question refers to the Messier numbers of these astronomical objects, according to the classification of nebulae, galaxies and star clusters devised by the French astronomer Charles Messier, the first version of which was published in 1774.

The Crab nebula is classified **M1**, and thus shares its designation with the motorway going from London to Leeds.

The Trifid nebula is **M20** – as is the motorway leading to Folkestone and the Channel Tunnel terminal.

The Orion nebula is classified **M42** – like the motorway that skirts the Birmingham conurbation to the south and east.

Q5

What might you make by mixing up: a former model and runner-up Miss USA who won an Oscar as a woman involved in an inter-racial relationship; a raw Swedish-born singer once dubbed 'The Black Madonna'; a film character who cares for his obese mother and autistic brother; and the Sicilian boss of an American crime family?

CLUES

- Getting any one of the ingredients of this question should give you the theme.
- The crime family is a real one – so it's not the Sopranos or the Corleones, for example.

Q6

What would a nocturnal hotel employee, an emoticon, the little gentleman in the black velvet waistcoat and someone seeking shelter in winter all be doing together in the Square?

CLUES

- These elements all belong to the same shadowy world.
- Thinking of the phrase 'the Square' in a foreign language might be helpful.

A5

A fruit salad.

They are: Halle **Berry** (b.1966), runner-up Miss USA 1986, winner of the Oscar for Best Actress in a Leading Role for *Monster's Ball* (2001) in which she played Leticia Musgrove; Neneh **Cherry**, born Neneh Mariann Karlsson in Stockholm in 1964, whose debut album *Raw Like Sushi* was a bestseller in 1989; Gilbert **Grape** – in the 1993 film *What's Eating Gilbert Grape?* starring Johnny Depp and Leonardo DiCaprio; and Joe **Bananas** (Joseph Bonanno, 1905–2002), American crime boss. Born in Sicily, he came to the United States illegally in 1924, settled in Brooklyn, and soon became a bootlegger and mob enforcer. In 1931 he founded the Bonanno crime family, one of five families that dominated organized crime in New York City. Bonanno's crime family, which he ruled until the mid-1960s, eventually extended from Brooklyn to Arizona, California and Canada and controlled such illegal enterprises as gambling, loan-sharking and drug trafficking.

A6

These are all clues to titles or elements associated with John le Carré ('the Square'), real name David Cornwell (b.1931).

The nocturnal hotel employee is ***The Night Manager***, as in le Carré's 1993 novel televised in 2016.

An emoticon would be a **Smiley** – the name of the protagonist in le Carré's classic sequence of novels including *Tinker Tailor Soldier Spy* (1974), *The Honourable Schoolboy* (1977) and *Smiley's People* (1979).

The little gentleman in black velvet is a **mole** – the reference being to the mole whose hole supposedly caused the Protestant King William III's horse Sorrel to fall and throw him off, in 1702. The king died of pneumonia arising from the fall, and Jacobites subsequently toasted 'the little gentleman in the black velvet waistcoat' who put an end to the rule of the House of Orange.

The seeker of shelter is a reference to ***The Spy Who Came in from the Cold*** (1963).

Q7

Why might you look for the lead singer of the Drifters in Glasgow, Detective Mary Beth Lacey in Newcastle and a Belgian international footballer in Carlisle?

CLUES

- Think of the geographical factors that are favourable for the location and growth of a city.
- If you can remember who played Detective Lacey, you're well on your way.

Q8

What have a cricket commentator, an architect, a French cypher, a Yorkshire power station and a point blank refusal done to upset an American ornithologist?

CLUES

- The ornithologist gave his name to someone else rather better known.
- New people emerge to upset him every few years, and there's no sign of an end to it yet.

A7

These people all have the names of rivers in northern Britain.

The original singer with the Drifters, in the mid-1950s, was the pioneering soul singer **Clyde** McPhatter (1932–72). After McPhatter left to pursue a solo career, the Drifters had one of the most notoriously fluid line-ups of any band, recording and touring for decades with an ever-shifting team of musicians. Glasgow, of course, is on the River Clyde.

Detective Mary Beth Lacey in the TV drama *Cagney & Lacey* was played by **Tyne** Daly (b.1946). Newcastle stands on the River Tyne.

The Belgian international midfielder is **Eden** Hazard – who joined Chelsea from Lille in 2012 and moved to Real Madrid in 2019. The River Eden runs through Carlisle.

A8

They are all adversaries of James Bond in the Ian Fleming novels and film adaptations. The name of Fleming's spy was allegedly inspired by the author of *Birds of the West Indies*, which Fleming had on his shelf at home in Jamaica.

The cricket commentator is Henry **Blofeld**, whose father was at Eton with Ian Fleming and whose surname Fleming took for the name of his arch villain Ernst Stavro Blofeld, first introduced in the novel *Thunderball* in 1961.

The Hungarian-born modernist architect Ernő **Goldfinger**'s name was borrowed for the villain Auric Goldfinger in, er, *Goldfinger*.

The French cypher is **Le Chiffre**, the sinister villain in Fleming's first Bond novel, *Casino Royale* – later played on screen by Peter Lorre (in the 1954 American TV version), Orson Welles (in the 1967 spoof) and Mads Mikkelsen (2006).

The Yorkshire power station is **Drax**, as in Sir Hugo Drax, the villain of *Moonraker*.

A flat refusal is **no** – as in Dr Julius No in *Dr No*.

Q9

Can you turn DeForest Kelley into the creator of Harry Hole, by way of some Welsh soap?

CLUES

- 'Some Welsh soap' is not a cutesy way of referring to a TV series.
- Once you've got one of the three, it just requires a bit of shuffling.

Q10

Why would a wild dog, a game of numbers, a hillock in permafrost, a foreign language and a drummer form a sequence – and in which order should they come?

CLUES

- Eyes down for this one.
- The sequence is purely about the words, and nothing to do with size or chronology.

A9

These are three anagrams, give or take a diacritical mark.

Bones – as in Dr Leonard 'Bones' McCoy, played by DeForest Kelley (1920–99) in the original *Star Trek* series in 1966–9 and in the first six *Star Trek* films.

Nesbo – as in Jo Nesbø (b.1960), Norwegian novelist and musician, whose series about detective Harry Hole has sold millions around the world since his novels began being published in English in 2006. Titles (in English translation) include *The Redbreast, Nemesis, The Devil's Star, The Redeemer, The Snowman* and *The Leopard*. He has also written successful children's books including *Doctor Proctor's Fart Powder* (2007) and is the frontman of the Norwegian rock band Di Derre.

Both of these are anagrams of ***sebon***, which is Welsh for soap.

A10

They are (in the order of the question) dingo, bingo, pingo, lingo and Ringo. You just have to sort them into alphabetical order.

A **dingo** (*Canis lupus dingo*) is a wild dog found mainly in Australia.

The game of numbers is **bingo**.

A **pingo**, also known as a hydrolaccolith, is a small hill found in Arctic and sub-Arctic landscapes such as Siberia, Alaska, northern Canada, Spitsbergen and Greenland. A pingo is formed by ground ice lifting the layer of earth on top of it into a mound which can be over a hundred feet in height. The Kadleroshilik Pingo in Alaska is the highest-known pingo in the world, rising 178 feet from the surrounding lake plain.

A foreign language is colloquially known as the local **lingo**.

The drummer is, needless to say, **Ringo** Starr (real name Richard Starkey, b.1940).

ROUND 22

Q1

On which island could you notionally find the captain of a ship, a Tennessee Williams character played by Brando, a ska trombonist, and a soldier at the bottom of the pecking order?

CLUES

- This is probably one for millennials.
- The captain is a general term for a captain, not a specific captain.

Q2

Which composer with Manchester and Orkney associations is connected with the father of quantum physics, a pioneer of movie make-up and a computer-generated talk-show host – and why would you struggle to turn them up any louder?

CLUES

- You're looking for a name common to all of them.
- The talk-show host – somewhat ahead of his time – dates from the 1980s.

A1

On Madagascar – because these are the names of the four penguins in the movie *Madagascar* and its sequels, who went on to star in a caper of their own in 2014.

The leader of the penguins (the 'sensible' one) is called **Skipper**.

Marlon Brando played Stanley **Kowalski** on Broadway and in the 1951 movie of Tennessee Williams's *A Streetcar Named Desire*. Kowalski is one of the most common of all Polish family names, being literally the equivalent of 'Smith'.

The late '**Rico**' Rodriguez (1934–2015) was one of the best known ska musicians in the UK, having moved there from Jamaica in 1961 and played with many influential bands including the Specials and Jools Holland.

The fourth penguin is called **Private**, the lowest rank of soldier in an army. The use of the phrase 'pecking order' might provide a further clue to the theme here.

A2

The composer is Sir Peter Maxwell Davies (1934–2016), the former Master of the Queen's Music, was always known to his friends as Max. The others are all connected, and can't be turned up, because they are all already 'Max'.

Born in Salford, **Sir Peter Maxwell Davies**'s career began as a teenager when he was spotted by the BBC in Manchester and given the job of regularly composing music for the radio show *Children's Hour*. He settled in Orkney in 1971, where the surroundings inspired much of his later music, and founded a music festival there.

Max Planck (1858–1947) formulated the quantum theory of electromagnetic energy, in 1900. Since the theory was not compatible with classical physical laws, it paved the way for quantum physics and a whole new approach to the theory of the universe. Planck won the Nobel Prize for Physics in 1918.

Max Factor Sr (Maximilian Faktorovich, 1877–1938), born in Łodz in Russian Poland, emigrated to the US in 1904 and made his name manufacturing wigs and stage make-up for the fledgling film industry – before his company turned into one of the world's leading cosmetics brands.

Max Headroom was a computer-generated host of a Channel 4 series first shown in 1985. The character was played by Matt Frewer and was supposedly synthesized from the memories of Edison Carter, the name 'Max Headroom' having been the last words Carter saw before a road accident plunged him into a coma. Computer technology wasn't advanced enough at the time to create a genuine computer-animated character for a TV series on this budget – so the illusion was created with prosthetic make-up. The show was mainly a vehicle for playing pop videos.

Q3

What pattern might you see in a Mad man, a Beryl Bainbridge novel and a school in Hertfordshire?

CLUES

- The word 'pattern' is not used randomly.
- See if you can stitch together the elements here.

Q4

What sacred number might connect Enid Blyton, George Axelrod, Akira Kurosawa, St Giles in the Fields and the cliffs of Sussex?

CLUES

- George Axelrod, the least familiar name here, is a playwright, one of whose works became a famous film.
- When you see this connection you'll think it's magnificent.

A3

Perhaps a pattern from which clothing is made – because these all have names pertaining to clothing.

A Mad man is Don **Draper**, played by Jon Hamm in the TV series *Mad Men*, the creative director of fictional Manhattan ad agency Sterling Cooper. Mad is short for Madison Avenue, where all of the ad agencies were headquartered in the 1950s. Draper's character is, apparently, at least partly inspired by a real-life ad executive called Draper Daniels.

One of the best known and most successful of the late Beryl Bainbridge's novels is ***The Dressmaker***, shortlisted for the 1973 Booker Prize. Macabre and semi-autobiographical, it's about a dressmaker and her sister in the north of England during the Second World War, who are looking after a teenage girl who's having a delusional relationship with an American soldier.

The school in Hertfordshire is the public school known as **Haberdashers'**, more fully Haberdashers' Aske's, in Elstree, founded in 1690 by a Royal Charter granted to the Worshipful Company of Haberdashers to establish a hospital for 20 boarders with funds from the legacy of the wealthy London cloth merchant Robert Aske.

A4

Seven: a number with mystical and ritual significance in many cultures and religions since ancient times.

Enid Blyton's 15 **Secret Seven** books, featuring the crime-solving adventures of a troupe of pre-teens, appeared between 1949 and 1963.

George Axelrod (1922–2003) wrote the play ***The Seven Year Itch*** (1952), which became the 1955 Billy Wilder film with Marilyn Monroe and Tom Ewell.

Akira Kurosawa's ***Seven Samurai*** (*Shichinin nō Samurai*, 1954) was adapted by Hollywood as *The Magnificent Seven* (1960).

The area of London known as **Seven Dials**, just off St Giles High Street, was named because a pillar stood at the apex of seven radiating streets at its heart, bearing sundials facing in each direction. (Curiously, in fact there were only ever six sundials on the pillar.) In the eighteenth and nineteenth centuries Seven Dials was a notorious den of vice, and became one of the worst slums of the Victorian city, as chronicled in the writings of Dickens and the art of Gustave Doré.

The chain of chalk cliffs along the Sussex Heritage Coast between Cuckmere Haven and Beachy Head is known as the **Seven Sisters**.

Q5

An Art Nouveau architect, a victorious Civil War leader and a Metropolitan Police Commissioner might all be said to betray epic ambitions: why?

CLUES

- Interestingly the word Metropolitan is important in the life of the architect, too.
- It may have been their parents who had ambitions *for* them, when they named them.

Q6

Why ought you to beware of *Haematopus ostralegus*, a coveted waterproof watch and bovine testicles, unless there's an R in the month?

CLUES

- Like most RBQ questions, it will take some effort to prise this one open.
- Familiarity with the theme here would once have meant you were quite poor, but it now suggests luxury.

A5

Because they all share forenames with people who feature in the story of the Trojan War.

The architect is **Hector** Guimard (1867–1942), French pioneer of the Art Nouveau style whose work includes the famous entrances and lettering of the Paris Metro stations.

The leader of the victorious Union army in the American Civil War was **Ulysses** S. Grant (1822–85), subsequently the eighteenth president of the USA.

Cressida Dick (b.1960) became the first ever female Commissioner of London's Metropolitan Police, and thus the UK's most senior police officer, in 2017.

A6

Because these all have an oyster connection: and the wisdom is that you should never eat an oyster unless there's an R in the month, meaning that you avoid them during the 'close season' between May and August.

Haematopus ostralegus is a wading bird, the common **oystercatcher**.

In developing the world's first waterproof watch the Rolex company founder Hans Wilsdorf named it an **oyster**, in reference to the watertight seal of an oyster's shell.

Cooked calves' testicles, eaten as a delicacy, are known as **prairie oysters**.

Q7

How would you once have gone about finding the phone numbers of the following?

CLUES

- The third picture is a self-portrait.
- The *name* of the particular cyclist here is not strictly relevant.

Q8

What might the first British Formula One champion, a jazz warrior and a senior conductor knighted in 2008 be doing in the countryside?

CLUES

- The Formula One champion is, sadly, a somewhat tragic figure.
- All of these people have grown on the British public over time.

A7

You'd probably (once upon a time, at least) have looked in the *Yellow Pages*.

The images depict: the Beatles in a promotional poster for the 1969 cartoon film ***Yellow*** *Submarine*; Geraint Thomas winning the 2018 Tour de France and thereby taking the **Yellow** Jersey; and a self-portrait by Aubrey Beardsley, who was closely associated with the racy and controversial 1890s periodical *The* ***Yellow*** *Book*.

A8

They might just be growing there – their names suggest three common native British species of tree.

Mike **Hawthorn** (1929–59) won the Formula One Drivers' Championship in 1958. His career was marred by his involvement in more than one race that ended fatally for another driver. He himself died tragically young in a car accident soon after his retirement.

The jazz warrior is Courtney **Pine** (b.1964), British jazz multi-instrumentalist, founder of the Jazz Warriors in the 1980s; he's an ambassador, broadcaster, popularizer and communicator as well as a performer of contemporary jazz.

Sir Mark **Elder** (b.1947) is one of Britain's foremost orchestral conductors, appointed Music Director of the Hallé Orchestra in Manchester in 1999, knighted for services to music in 2008 and appointed a Companion of Honour in 2017.

Q9

If you wanted to find some youths who'd do favours for you at a public school, an assassinated San Francisco politician, and two waltzes by Offenbach and Johann Strauss II, why might you go and see Tjinder Singh?

CLUES

- You're looking for some everyday objects here.
- The politician has been the subject of a film.

Q10

How would you classify a horny structure in a horse's hoof, a child traumatized by aliens and a tense Belgian crime drama?

CLUES

- There is a connection with the animal kingdom throughout.
- Would it make it slightly easier to give Aliens a capital letter?

A9

Because Tjinder Singh is the creative genius behind the band Cornershop – and these all suggest items you would pick up at the corner shop.

Fags are boys who traditionally did menial jobs for senior pupils at English public schools.

The assassinated politician was the openly gay San Francisco legislative official Harvey **Milk**, shot dead with the city's Mayor George Moscone in November 1978 by a grudgeful fellow official.

The two waltzes by Offenbach and Strauss, composed in 1863 for a ball organized by the Vienna Authors and Journalists' Association, were respectively given the names 'Abendblätter' and 'Morgenblätter' (**'Evening Papers'** and **'Morning Papers'**).

A10

You would classify them as amphibians because they are a frog, a Newt and a Salamander.

A **frog** is a triangular horny structure in the underside of a horse's hoof.

Newt is the human child struck dumb by terror, discovered and befriended by Ripley (Sigourney Weaver) after everyone else in her colony has been killed by aliens in the James Cameron sci-fi classic *Aliens* (1986). She was played by Carrie Henn.

The crime drama series ***Salamander***, starring Filip Peeters as Police Inspector Paul Gerardi, was first broadcast in 2012.

ROUND 23

Q1

A British actress who has played Condoleezza Rice and an android; a German-born photographer of monochrome nudes; and a slave ship captain who became an abolitionist and hymn writer: why might they all feel the weight of their forebears' reputation?

CLUES

- With a bit of thought you'll gravitate to the right solution.
- This question was topical around the time of series 4 of the TV series *Line of Duty*.

Q2

Can you make the following rhyme: *Ruslan and Lyudmila*, Rodin's *Poet*, Smollett's Humphry and the people of Atahualpa?

CLUES

- Rodin's *Poet* is better known by a different description.
- They wouldn't all rhyme if an American English speaker said them.

A1

They might feel the weight because they are all named Newton; and weight is measured in newtons, the SI unit of force, named after the British scientist Sir Isaac Newton.

Cambridge-educated British actress **Thandie Newton** (b.1972) played Condoleezza Rice in *W*, Oliver Stone's biopic of George W. Bush, and has more recently won awards for her role as the android Maeve Millay in the sci-fi TV drama *Westworld*. She was also DCI Roz Huntley in series 4 of Jed Mercurio's *Line of Duty*.

Photographer **Helmut Newton** (1920–2004) became best known for his fetishistic fashion photographs and iconic nudes, often in black and white.

John Newton (1725–1807) was press-ganged into the Royal Navy at the age of 18 and worked on slave ships before a religious conversion led to his being ordained and eventually working with William Wilberforce to achieve the abolition of slavery. He wrote a great many religious poems and hymns, including the words of 'Amazing Grace'.

A2

The rhyming sound here is '-inka', and the phrases in the question give us Glinka, Thinker, Clinker and Inca. (Clearly, these are not all satisfactory rhymes in American English.)

Ruslan and Lyudmila is an opera by Mikhail Ivanovich **Glinka** to a libretto by Valerian Fyodorovich Shirkov (with minor contributions by others) after Pushkin's 1820 poem, first performed in St Petersburg in 1842.

When conceived in 1880 in its original size (approx. 70 cm) as the crowning element of *The Gates of Hell*, Rodin's *The* **Thinker** was entitled *The Poet*. He represented Dante, author of the *Divine Comedy*, leaning forward to observe the circles of Hell. While remaining in place on the monumental Gates of Hell, *The Thinker* was exhibited individually in 1888 and thus became an independent work. Enlarged in 1904, its colossal version proved even more popular.

The Expedition of Humphry **Clinker** is an epistolary novel by Tobias Smollett, published in three volumes in 1771, the year of his death.

Atahualpa (*c.*1502–33), thirteenth and last emperor of the **Inca**, was executed by Spanish conquistador Francisco Pizarro in 1533 – marking the end of the Inca empire.

Q3

In what way can an instrumental no. 1 hit of 1960, the capital city of Wyoming, a military helicopter and several light aircraft be said to commemorate the subjugated?

CLUES

- You may need native wit to see the theme here.
- Not just the Wyoming bit, but all of it, has to do with the American West.

Q4

Why might you find all of the following at Ninus's tomb: a woodwind instrument, the fruit of *Cydonia oblonga*, an animal's nose, anyone's hindquarters, an undernourished person, and a cosy corner of a pub?

CLUES

- It would be rude to imply you needed more help with this one.
- You're looking for the names of six people who all do something together.

A3

This is about the names of Native American tribes, subjugated and depleted by white expansion and conquest, and by foreign diseases, since the first European settlement of the Americas.

The instrumental hit is **'Apache'**, composed by Jerry Lordan, which became the first no. 1 for the Shadows (after an unsuccessful initial recording by Bert Weedon). Lordan cited as his inspiration for the melody the 1954 Western film *Apache,* starring Burt Lancaster.

Cheyenne is the capital city of Wyoming. Native American names for towns, rivers and other geographical features are an ever-present reminder of the history of the territories concerned.

The instantly recognizable twin-engine Boeing **Chinook** helicopter is one of the workhorses of the US Army and the Royal Air Force, introduced in 1962.

The Florida-based Piper aircraft company made a point of naming its models after Native American tribes in the 1950s and 60s: the **Pawnee** was followed by the **Comanche**, the **Cherokee,** the **Apache**, the **Navajo** and the **Cheyenne**.

A4

They'd be at Ninus's tomb because that's the setting for the play about Pyramus and Thisbe performed by the 'rude mechanicals' in Shakespeare's *A Midsummer Night's Dream.*

The mechanicals in the play are **Flute** (a woodwind instrument), **Quince** (a fruit), **Snout** (an animal's nose), **Bottom** (hindquarters), **Starveling** (an undernourished person) and **Snug** (a cosy corner of a pub).

Q5

In which book would you be most likely to find together: a British journalist and thriller writer who debuted with *Alys, Always*; an Australian multiple Grand-Slam-winning tennis star, now a Christian minister; an actor who found fame as the original bunny-boiler; and Perry Mason's loyal secretary?

CLUES

- Address yourself carefully to this question.
- Any or all of them could quite feasibly be in your town.

Q6

A royal performer set out his stall by confessing to impure thoughts, before excitedly anticipating the end of a century, then followed it up with some colourful precipitation and a rapid circumnavigation of the globe, before lamenting the state of the age, soundtracking a superhero and garlanding himself with jewels – and all this before a symbol took over. Who is this about?

CLUES

- The performer is royal in name only.
- If we told you the colour of the precipitation you'd get it straight away, because this colour is indelibly associated with him.

A5

The answer is the *A to Z*, or any kind of street atlas, because they are women whose full names sound like addresses.

Harriet Lane, British author born in 1969; **Margaret Court** (b.1942), one of the very few women to have won every one of the major Grand Slam tennis titles – in singles, doubles and mixed doubles – during her career; **Glenn Close** (b.1947), whose superstardom came after *Fatal Attraction* (1987) in which her character Alex has an affair and then a murderous feud with Dan (Michael Douglas); **Della Street**, the glamorous fictional secretary of attorney Perry Mason in the stories by Erle Stanley Gardner (1889–1970).

A6

The royal performer is Prince (1958–2016).

Well done if you spotted the reference to seven album titles.

Confessing to impure thoughts (***Dirty Mind***), before excitedly anticipating the end of a century (***1999***), then some colourful precipitation (***Purple Rain***) and a rapid circumnavigation of the globe (***Around the World in a Day***), before lamenting the state of the age (***Sign o' the Times***), soundtracking a superhero (***Batman***) and garlanding himself with jewels (***Diamonds and Pearls***). And all this before he changed his name to an unpronounceable symbol, in 1992.

Q7

Why might John Wilmot, William Pitt and John Montagu have been courted by the Conqueror?

CLUES

- These people all had aristocratic titles that are relevant.
- John Montagu is known for inventing a foodstuff without which modern life would be very different.

Q8

Which Goodie would flourish in the company of an Australian cricketing legend, a Colossal Tunny-hunter and a giant of German post-war literature?

CLUES

- By 'Goodie' we mean a member of the Goodies.
- The work of the Tunny-hunter was top secret but led to the development of a vital component of twenty-first-century life.

A7

They are, respectively, the real names of the Earl of Rochester, the Earl of Chatham and the Earl of Sandwich – all 'Men of Kent' (i.e. from the lands east of the Medway). In opposition to the 'Kentish men' of the western half of the county, the Men of Kent were regarded as stout-hearted native stock, and granted many privileges by the Normans.

John Wilmot (1647–80) was the 2nd Earl of **Rochester**, by some distance the filthiest of all major English poets, author of 'Signior Dildo', 'The Imperfect Enjoyment' and other verses for all the family.

William Pitt the Elder (1708–78), aka 'The Great Commoner', was created 1st Earl of **Chatham** on his appointment as Lord Privy Seal in July 1766, although this, ironically, effectively ended his career, as he was no longer seen to live up to his nickname and thereby lost much of his popularity.

John Montagu (1718–92), the 4th Earl of **Sandwich,** gave his name to the dish of meat and bread he is alleged to have invented around 1762, to eat during a 24-hour stint at a gaming table. He was a member of Francis Dashwood's dissolute 'Hellfire Club' or the 'Mad Monks of Medmenham Abbey'. Captain Cook named the Sandwich Islands (now Hawaii) after him.

A8

This is about people with horticultural names.

Dr Graeme **Garden** (b.1943) was one of the Goodies, as well as having been a writer and performer at the heart of the British comedy establishment since the mid-1960s. He has been a resident panellist on Radio 4's *I'm Sorry I Haven't a Clue* since 1972 and he co-devised *The Unbelievable Truth* with Jon Naismith.

Allan **Border** (b.1955), Australian cricket captain, held the world record for consecutive Test appearances (153) until 2018 when it was surpassed by Alastair Cook.

Tommy **Flowers**, MBE (1905–98) led the hunt to crack the Nazis' Tuna or Tunny code, several orders of magnitude more complex than Enigma. He was recommended by Alan Turing and he worked at Dollis Hill (the Post Office's research centre) during the war years, producing a valve-driven proto-computer known as Colossus, which he demonstrated at Bletchley Park in December 1943.

The oeuvre of the prolific German novelist Günter **Grass** (1927–2015) includes some of the most important works of post-war German self-examination and rehabilitation. *Die Blechtrommel* (*The Tin Drum*, 1959) is his most famous book.

Q9

If you'd arranged to meet a Devon poet and critic, Alan Measles's best friend and the rapper Tracy Lauren Marrow in a bar, what would you order for them?

CLUES

- The poet is one of the foremost British women poets of the late twentieth century.
- The rapper has a strong interest in heavy metal music.

Q10

Ralph Fiennes as Charles van Doren; James McAvoy as Brian Jackson; and Dev Patel as Jamal Malik. What do they have in common?

CLUES

- The fact that these people have a quiz question devoted to them seems very appropriate.
- Don't make this one seem harder than it really is.

A9

You'd line up drinks on the bar appropriate to their names.

The English poet and critic from Devon is Patricia **Beer** (1919–99).

Alan Measles's best friend is the British artist Grayson **Perry** (b.1960). Alan Measles is his teddy bear, with him since childhood, whom he sometimes carries with him in public and who appears occasionally in his work.

Tracy Lauren Marrow (b.1958) is the real name of the rapper known as **Ice-T.**

A10

They are the protagonists in three movies about quizzes.

Ralph Fiennes starred as disgraced contestant Charles van Doren who was 'fed' the answers in Robert Redford's film ***Quiz Show*** (1994), about the *Twenty-One* quiz-fixing scandal of 1950s America.

James McAvoy is the gauche hero of ***Starter for 10***, (dir. Tom Vaughan, 2006) based on the novel by David Nicholls, who succumbs to the ultimate temptation on *University Challenge*.

Dev Patel plays the young contestant Jamal Malik from the shanties of Mumbai, forced to defend his extraordinary performance on *Who Wants to Be a Millionaire*, in Danny Boyle's glorious ***Slumdog Millionaire*** (2008), loosely adapted from the novel *Q&A* by Vikas Swarup.

ROUND 24

The last two quizzes showcase some of the very best questions received in recent years from *Round Britain Quiz* listeners. Listeners' ideas these days come in from all over the world: they are often much cleverer than the ones we think of ourselves, and they have been an essential feature of the broadcasts for decades.

Q1

From Peter Vigurs

Why might a liberated Australian-born DJ from the 1960s, after a brush with Mary O'Brien and Sandra Goodrich, feel uneasy about a visit from the thirty-first president of the USA?

CLUES

- 'Liberated' is a clue to the DJ's name, not necessarily his lifestyle.
- The two women are singers, but not widely known by those names.

Q2

From Dave Taylor

What egotistical addition can transform: a citizen of 'no mean city' into a quantum physicist; a Berkshire dessert into an international soccer superstar; and split peas into the creator of an aphrodisiac telephone?

CLUES

- 'No mean city' is a phrase from the Bible.
- The soccer superstar is Argentinian.

A1

Because the 'liberated' DJ is Alan Freeman (1927–2006), universally known as Fluff ...

His 'brush' with Mary O'Brien and Sandra Goodrich would have brought him into contact (respectively) with 1960s singers **Dusty** Springfield and **Sandie** Shaw ...

And they might all therefore feel nervous about a visit from Herbert **Hoover**.

A2

The letter 'i': so that (St) Paul becomes (Wolfgang) Pauli; (Eton) mess becomes (Lionel) Messi; Dal becomes (Salvador) Dalí.

In the Book of Acts, ch. 21, **Paul** refers to himself as 'a Jew from Tarsus, in Cilicia, a citizen of no mean city'. Wolfgang **Pauli** (1900–58), Austrian-born physicist, received the 1945 Nobel Prize for Physics for his discovery in 1925 of the Pauli exclusion principle, which states that in an atom no two electrons can occupy the same quantum state simultaneously. Pauli made major contributions to quantum mechanics, quantum field theory and solid-state physics, and he successfully hypothesized the existence of the neutrino.

Eton **Mess** is traditionally chopped strawberries macerated in kirsch, then mixed with whipped cream and crushed meringue, and decorated with strawberries and mint. Lionel **Messi** (b.1987) is the legendary Argentine-born football player whose family relocated to Barcelona so he could play with the youth team at the age of 13. In 2005 he was granted Spanish citizenship, an honour greeted with mixed feelings by the fiercely Catalan supporters of Barcelona. The next year Messi and Barcelona won the Champions League title.

Dal is a traditional Indian dish made from the split pulses: peas, lentils or beans. Salvador **Dalí** (1904–89), the Spanish surrealist painter, created the hybrid of a Bakelite telephone and a lobster, to which he gave the title *Aphrodisiac Telephone*, in 1936.

Q3

From Dr Mario Brown

Add Punjab; Szechuan; and Truro. How many, and of what, do you have in total?

CLUES

- It will help to know what any (or all) of these place names mean.
- If you give up on this, move on, it's water under the bridge.

Q4

From Martin Rowson

Can you find the odd one out between Agamemnon, Marat, Jim Morrison and Marion Crane?

CLUES

- Marion Crane is a fictional character, very famous but rather short-lived.
- The best known surviving visual image of Marat gives you a heavy clue.

A3

Twelve – rivers. The names of these places all refer to a specific number of rivers.

Punjab means **'five rivers'** (*panj*, five + *aab*, water).

Szechuan means **'four rivers'** (its full name literally means 'the four circuits of rivers and gorges').

Truro means **'three rivers'** (from Cornish *tri-veru*). They are the Truro river, the Kenwyn and the Allen.

A4

They all died in the bath – except for Marion Crane, who died in the *shower.*

In Aeschylus's *Oresteia*, **Agamemnon**, the hero of Troy, is bludgeoned to death in his bath by Clytemnestra.

Jean-Paul Marat was killed in his bath in July 1793 by the fanatical Charlotte Corday, as portrayed in the painting by his friend Jacques-Louis David depicting Marat's pallid corpse clutching the letter of introduction he received from her. Translated it reads: 'Citizen, my extreme misery is enough to warrant me your benevolence'. It's in the Musées Royaux des Beaux-Arts, Brussels.

Jim Morrison (1943–71), flamboyant and troubled singer with the American rock group the Doors, was found dead in his bath in Paris on 3 July 1971 after a whirlwind five-year orgy of rock 'n' roll fame, drugs, drink, theatricality, exhibitionism, imprisonment and meaningless poetry. He was buried in Père Lachaise Cemetery and his grave has become a site of pilgrimage.

Marion Crane is the character played by Janet Leigh in the Hitchcock horror classic *Psycho* (1960), knifed to death in graphic monochrome by Norman Bates (Anthony Perkins) as she takes a shower in her motel room.

Q5

From Kieran Sidley

Why could Philip Pirrip, a short, high-pitched cry and the saint who told us how we should calculate Easter all have been seen by our grandparents in the mirror?

CLUES

- Philip Pirrip occurred elsewhere in the book in a question about palindromes. That has nothing to do with it this time.
- We could have helped you by giving the Mirror a capital letter.

Q6

From Peter Cole

Can you proceed, in a random fashion, from a creature of dual gender, via a technique of Renaissance painting, to an Italian-sounding instrument?

CLUES

- This is an ingenious etymological connection.
- It's a question of contrasts.

A5

Because the clues give us *Pip, Squeak & Wilfred* – which was a long-running cartoon strip published in the *Daily Mirror* in 1919–53. The names are those of three animal characters, a dog, a penguin and a baby rabbit. Pip, Squeak & Wilfred were also the nicknames given to the First World War medals the British War Medal, the Victory Medal and either the 1914 or the 1914–15 Star.

The protagonist and narrator Philip Pirrip is known as **Pip** in Dickens's *Great Expectations* (1861).

A high-pitched cry is a **Squeak**.

St **Wilfrid** (634–*c.*710) advocated the lunar calculation of the date of Easter. Born in Northumbria of noble parentage, he was educated at Lindisfarne and Canterbury. With Benedict Biscop he travelled to Lyons and Rome in 654; on returning to England in 661 he became abbot of Ripon. Moved by Wilfrid's eloquence, King Oswy at the Synod of Whitby (663/664) rejected Celtic usages, including the old reckoning of Easter, and established instead the Roman custom.

A6

This is about words or phrases that contain opposites.

'In a random fashion' is **willy-nilly** ('will he, nill he', alt. from Latin *Volui, nolui*, will I or won't I).

A creature of dual gender is a **hermaphrodite** (from the combination of the names of Hermes and Aphrodite in the pantheon of Greek gods).

A Renaissance painting technique is **chiaroscuro** (Italian *chiaro, oscuro*, light and shade).

The instrument is a **pianoforte** (which literally means 'soft-loud').

Q7

From Chris Channing

Shirley refused and Doris wavered; but a blonde and a brunette accepted – all of them repeatedly. How so, and who are they?

CLUES

- The theme of this question is musical, or rather, lyrical.
- Intriguingly, the first two did so in translation, and the blonde and brunette weren't actually using their native language.

Q8

From David Barnes

If the answer is the national bird of India, with Hitchcock's first film in colour, in the domain of Demetrius of Phaleron, what game are we playing?

CLUES

- The subject matter of the Hitchcock film is not unconnected with the overall theme.
- Demetrius of Phaleron lived and worked in ancient Alexandria.

A7

Shirley Bassey, Doris Day and ABBA's Agnetha and Frida did so via song titles.

'Never Never Never' was Shirley Bassey's 1973 hit cover of the Tony Renis Italian hit 'Grande Grande Grande'. Italian singer Mina also had success with it in the early 1970s.

Doris Day was one of many people to cover **'Perhaps Perhaps Perhaps'**, the English version of the 1947 Cuban song 'Quizas Quizas Quizas' by Osvaldo Farrés. The English lyrics were written by Joe Davis, the record producer who convinced Fats Waller to start performing.

'I do, I do, I do, I do, I do' by ABBA (the singers being Agnetha Fältskog and Frida Lyngstad) was the single that led to ABBA fever in Australia. It didn't do too well in the UK, however, only scraping the top 40 in 1975 and leading many to assume they had been a mere Eurovision flash-in-the-pan.

A8

Cluedo.

The national bird of India is the **Peacock**, *Pavo cristatus*.

The Hitchcock film is ***Rope*** (1948), Hitchcock's first film in colour, inspired by the true story of two wealthy Chicago teenagers who murdered a younger boy just to see whether they could pull it off. John Dall and Farley Granger play the murderers, and James Stewart stars as the philosophy professor whose discursions on Nietzsche inspire them to commit the crime.

The Royal **Library** at Alexandria, the most famous library of classical antiquity, was organized by Demetrius of Phaleron.

This gives us the possible Cluedo solution 'Mrs Peacock, with the Rope, in the Library'.

Q9

From Juha Sorva

Whose enemies might have cause to fear the Nike logo, Duncan Jones, the son of a Salesman, a captured soldier and one of a pair of garments?

CLUES

- Let's not fight if you don't get the answer.
- Imagine a lot of exclamation marks after all of these things.

Q10

From James Heafield

Why ought you to ask permission from Mum and Dad before taking tea with primates, sending an email to an Oceanic domain or reading the works of Plum?

CLUES

- Initially you might find this baffling.
- The primates in question are chimpanzees. Does this help?

A9

Batman, as they all relate to words used in Bat-fights.

The Nike logo is called the **Swoosh**, Duncan Jones – son of David Bowie – was formerly known as **Zowie** Bowie, the son of Willy Loman in Arthur Miller's play *Death of a Salesman* is **Biff**, a captured soldier is a **POW** and the garment is a **sock**.

DC Comics' superhero Batman was created in 1939 by illustrator Bob Kane and writer Bill Finger. In the 1960s the *Batman* television series starring Adam West adopted the cartoon-strip tradition of having captions carrying the words 'POW!', 'BIFF!', etc. punctate the action during fight scenes.

Nike, Inc. was founded in 1964 as Blue Ribbon Sports by Bill Bowerman, a track-and-field coach at the University of Oregon, and his former student Phil Knight. They launched the Nike brand shoe in 1972. The company was renamed Nike, Inc. in 1978 and went public two years later.

Duncan Jones was born on 30 May 1971 in Bromley as Duncan Zowie Haywood Jones, to David Bowie and his then-wife Angie. He is a director and writer, known for *Moon* (2009), *Source Code* (2011) and *Warcraft: The Beginning* (2016).

Biff is the elder son of Willy Loman, who feuds with his father and dares to puncture his dreams, in *Death of a Salesman* (1949).

A10

They are all PGs. You would in theory require Mum and Dad's permission because PG indicates Parental Guidance.

Taking tea with primates should – at least for a certain generation – instantly call to mind the **PG Tips** chimpanzees, drafted in from Twycross Zoo for the Brooke Bond tea company's TV adverts between 1956 and 2002. The most popular was probably the 'Mr Shifter' scenario involving chimps dressed as removal men. The ad campaign was a huge success and PG Tips became a market leader, despite protests from animal rights groups. At one time the daily chimps' tea-parties were a huge attraction at Twycross Zoo, though it was always hard to tell whether the chimps taking part were the actual TV stars.

The internet country code top-level domain (ccTLD) for Papua New Guinea is **.pg**.

'Plum' is **P. G. Wodehouse** (1881–1975) – the nickname was a childhood contraction of his first given name 'Pelham' which remained current among family and friends for his lifetime.

ROUND 25

Q1

From Ivan Whetton

Why could a Northern Irish tenor, the first conductor of *The Planets* and the lawyer who wrote the words of the American national anthem make you feel more secure?

CLUES

- The tenor was the subject of a film.
- Find the link and it will all open up.

Q2

From Bruford Low

Cut the following in half, put them in the correct order and identify what is missing: a fairy-tale opening, a stripper trying to earn Rent, a dead bird, an island race, somewhere you can find a piano-playing Gosling, and something neither good nor bad.

CLUES

- In the scale of difficulty, this one is relatively straightforward.
- The piano-playing Gosling could play you the solution.

A1

Because their names give us a Lock(e), a Bo(u)lt and a Key.

Tenor **Josef Locke** was born Joseph McLaughlin in 1917 in Derry, the son of a butcher and cattle dealer, and one of nine children. He became a well-loved performer of sentimental and traditional Irish songs in British music halls, on radio and in films in the 1940s and 1950s, and his story was told in the 1991 film *Hear My Song*.

The eminent English conductor**, Sir Adrian Cedrik Boult** (1889–1983) was one of the twentieth century's greatest British conductors and a noted champion of British music. He was the first, and probably still best-known, conductor of Holst's *The Planets*. He was appointed Director of Music by the BBC in 1930 and founded the BBC Symphony Orchestra. He was associated with the Philharmonia, the Royal Philharmonic Orchestra and, most famously, the London Symphony Orchestra.

Francis Scott Key (1779–1843) was an American lawyer and poet. After witnessing events of the Battle of Baltimore in September 1814, Key wrote a poem he called 'The Defence of Fort M'Henry', whose words were set to a popular melody by John Stafford Smith and became famous as 'The Star-Spangled Banner'.

A2

Halved and put in order, these give you Do – Mi – Fa – So – La – Te, the notes of the tonic Sol-fa. So missing is Re (the second note).

Far far (away) – a popular opening for fairy tales; **Mimi** – a character in the musical *Rent* (and the opera *La Bohème* which inspired it); **dodo** – a dead (as in extinct) bird; **TT** – a motorcycle race held on the Isle of Man; *La La Land* – a film in which Ryan Gosling plays a jazz pianist; **so-so** – neither good nor bad.

Q3

From James Tween

One was a president honoured for seeking 'peaceful solutions to international conflicts'; another silenced a King who had received the same honour; and the third gave voice to a different king ... though he's better known as a Lord. In conclusion, they vary, but who are they?

CLUES

- The one who silenced a King did so violently.
- The president we're looking for is the thirty-ninth.

Q4

From James Rutherford

How might a legendary firefighter, an Islamic festival and a case of the winter blues engender articles in *Der Spiegel*?

CLUES

- This is very carefully and cleverly worded: 'engender articles' has a double meaning.
- The German language is also important.

A3

People called James Earl ... respectively Carter, Ray and Jones. 'In conclusion' their names are different but they all begin the same way.

President **James Earl 'Jimmy' Carter,** thirty-ninth president of the USA, in office from 1977 to 1980, was awarded the Nobel Peace Prize in 2002 'for his decades of untiring effort to find peaceful solutions to international conflicts, to advance democracy and human rights, and to promote economic and social development'.

James Earl Ray (1928–98) pleaded guilty to murdering Martin Luther King in Memphis in 1968, though he later retracted his confession. King had been awarded the Nobel Peace Prize in 1964.

James Earl Jones voiced Mufasa in Disney's *The Lion King* (1994 and 2019) but is better known for voicing the Sith Lord Darth Vader in the *Star Wars* films.

A4

***Der Spiegel* translates as 'the mirror', and the three answers are the three definite *articles* in German associated with *gender*, but spelt backwards as in a mirror.**

The fireman is **Red** Adair – **Der**; the Islamic festival is **Eid** – **Die**; and the winter blues are known as **SAD** (Seasonal Affective Disorder) – **Das**.

Der Spiegel is a weekly news magazine, preeminent in Germany and one of the most widely circulated in Europe, published in Hamburg since 1947.

Red Adair (Paul Neal Adair, 1915–2004) was an American firefighter whose international reputation was established in 1962 when his team extinguished the 'Devil's Cigarette Lighter', a gas fire that had been raging in the desert of Algeria for six months. His teams were credited with fighting more than 2,000 fires in his career, including the 1988 Piper Alpha disaster in the North Sea. In 1991 Adair was asked to help cap the oil fires set by Iraqi troops fleeing Kuwait. Although it was thought that controlling these fires would take years to accomplish, Adair's team capped 117 wells and aided other teams in completing the job in eight months. Adair retired from firefighting in 1994.

ʿĪd al-Fiṭr, also spelled **Eid al-Fitr** (Arabic: festival of breaking fast) marks the end of Ramadan, the Muslim holy month of fasting, and is celebrated during the first three days of Shawwal, the tenth month of the Islamic calendar (though the Muslim use of a lunar calendar means that it may fall in any season of the year).

Seasonal Affective Disorder (SAD), a mood disorder characterized by recurring depression in autumn and winter, was first described in 1984 by the American psychiatrist Norman Rosenthal.

Q5

From Barbara Jennings

Which Welsh baritone, pompous fictional surgeon and Wilkie Collins villain could be considered appropriate members of a charitable social club?

CLUES

- It would be an honour to answer this excellent question.
- You may remember the surgeon as portrayed by James Robertson Justice.

Q6

From Roger Gill

Joyce's particular unintended progeny include: two that are vertical directions, two that are likeable and unusual, and two you might find written on a packing case. What are they – and why would you find them crossing the Swiss-French border very quickly?

CLUES

- It won't take you long to get the flavour of this question.
- You might work out the answers but you will almost certainly never see them.

A5

The charitable social club is the Round Table – named after that of Arthurian legend – and the three people in the clue are all knights, real or fictional, with appropriate Arthurian names.

Sir Geraint Evans (1922–92), much-loved Welsh operatic baritone/bass-baritone, was considered one of the greatest-ever Falstaffs (helped by his memorably whiskered, larger-than-life, Shakespearean appearance).

Sir Lancelot Spratt (memorably played by James Robertson Justice) was the domineering senior surgeon in the films of Richard Gordon's 'Doctor' books, starting with *Doctor in the House* (1954). Dirk Bogarde played Simon Sparrow.

Sir Percival Glyde is the villainous husband of Laura and associate of the vile Count Fosco in *The Woman in White* (1860). He and Fosco plot to have the blameless Laura locked up in an asylum, in place of the deranged but conveniently similar-looking woman of the title – so as to make people believe she has died and thus inherit her wealth. Needless to say, the plot unravels.

A6

They are quarks – the fundamental particles whose existence was proposed by the late American physicist Murray Gell-Mann, and named in 1964 after a phrase in James Joyce's *Finnegans Wake*, 'three quarks for Muster Mark'. Quarks make up hadrons, the particles being fired across (or rather, under) the Swiss-French border by the Large Hadron Collider, at speeds approaching that of light.

The question refers to six of the types or 'flavours' of quark. The two vertical directions are **Up** and **Down**; the likeable unusual ones are **Charm** and **Strange**; the packing case instructions are **Top** and **Bottom**.

Q7

From Bob Salmon

What do a nebulous approach to computing, Ray Bolger's stuffing, Boston's airport and 37.5 gallons of herring have to do with a culinary heroine who often used to be seen near Hollywood?

CLUES

- With luck your mental effort could prove fruitful here.
- Bob Salmon's own name could be another ingredient in this question.

Q8

From Roland Howell

One of Byron's daughters, with a change to the last vowel, becomes a Miltonic poetical character; and, with a further change to the same vowel, becomes one whose composition for the Sistine Chapel was written down by a visiting musician. Can you explain?

CLUES

- A lively mind is required for this.
- Less poetically, the second of these was an unloved model of motor car in the 1970s.

A7

The clues all lead to words that can be followed by Berry.

Cloud computing is a method of storing data in central computer systems and providing users access to them through the internet. **Cloudberries** are golden-yellow fruit, similar in shape to blackberries and ripening at a similar time of year, especially prevalent in northern climates and a common feature of Scandinavian desserts.

The best known screen role of American entertainer Ray Bolger (1904–87) is the Scarecrow in *The Wizard of Oz* (1939) who, being stuffed with **straw**, has no brain. A **strawberry** needs no explanation.

General Edward Lawrence **Logan** International Airport is the main airport serving metropolitan Boston, Massachusetts. It was named in 1943 after an officer in the Spanish-American War who came from Boston. The **loganberry** is a cross between raspberry and blackberry varieties originally produced by accident by the horticulturalist James Harvey Logan in California in 1883.

A **cran** is a unit of capacity used for measuring fresh herring, equal to 37.5 gallons. **Cranberries** are widely cultivated in boggy areas of the northern hemisphere, prized as a 'superfood' for their high antioxidant and vitamin C content.

Mary Berry (b.1935) has been a prominent cook and food writer since the 1960s, and found a whole new level of fame (and the status of national treasure) in her late seventies, as a judge alongside Paul Hollywood in the TV series *The Great British Bake Off* (BBC 2010–16).

A8

The sequence is Allegra – Allegro – Allegri.

Allegra, born 12 January 1817, was the illegitimate daughter of Lord Byron and Claire Clairmont, Mary Shelley's stepsister.

'L'Allegro', a poem published in 1645 by John Milton along with its companion piece 'Il Penseroso' – they mean, in opposition, 'the cheerful/lively one' and 'the pensive one'.

Gregorio **Allegri** (1582–1652), priest, tenor, and composer, is best known for the famous *Miserere* (the setting of Psalm 50 in the Roman Catholic enumeration), for nine voices, written for the Sistine Chapel where he worked for the later part of his life. The work was the exclusive property of the Sistine Chapel, and papal pronouncement strictly prohibited the reproduction of the score; but according to popular legend the 14-year-old Mozart was visiting Rome with his father, committed it to memory on the spot, and wrote it down subsequently, thus ensuring its immortality.

Q9

From Peter Stockdale

Three men were prepared to make a run for it, but only one did. Repeatedly, they have been used in messaging, seen in the African bush and heard in a mantra. Can you explain who, or what, they are?

CLUES

- The three men have names that form a familiar trio.
- There's a Second World War connection.

Q10

From Richard Humm

Which League, with 118 members so far, is this?
Germany 1, England 0
America 1, France 2
University of California 2, Russia 1
Stockholm 1, Suburb of Stockholm 4
Sunday Night! 1, Friday 1
Planets 4, Dwarf Planets 2

CLUES

- It's tempting to provide no clues to this splendid question: it's likely it will either baffle you completely or seem elementary.
- That's all you get.

A9

Tom, Dick and Harry were the nicknames of the three tunnels, 'prepared' as an escape route from Stalag Luft III, as portrayed in the film *The Great Escape* (1963), adapted by James Clavell and W. R. Burnett from the book by Paul Brickhill. In the event only Harry was used in the break-out.

'Repeatedly', they give us: a **tom-tom** – a type of African drum traditionally used to convey messages; a **dik-dik** – a dwarf antelope, of the genus *Madoqua*, found in eastern Africa; **Hare-Hare** – recited as a part of the mantra or chant of the Hare Krishna movement, in full the International Society of Krishna Consciousness (ISKCON), founded in the United States in 1965 by A. C. Bhaktivedanta.

As an aside, there was also a fourth tunnel – George – believed to have been begun in September 1944, before the arrival of freezing conditions in winter that would have made digging impossible.

A10

This is all to do with the Periodic Table of Chemical Elements and the places after which elements are named.

Germany 1, England 0 – Germany has **Germanium** (Ge, atomic no. 32), while England has no element named for the country.

America 1, France 2 – **Americium** (Am, 95); France has **Francium** (Fr, 87) and **Gallium** (Ga, 31).

University of California 2, Russia 1 – **Californium** (Cf, 98) and **Berkelium** (Bk, 97), while Russia is Ruthenia in Latin, hence **Ruthenium** (Ru, 44).

Stockholm 1, Suburb of Stockholm 4 – Stockholm has **Holmium** (Ho, 67), while, believe it or not, Ytterby, a small mine nearby, has **Yttrium** (Y, 39), **Ytterbium** (Yb, 70), **Terbium** (Tb, 65) and **Erbium** (Er, 68).

Sunday Night! 1, Friday 1 – Sunday night gave us **Palladium** (Pd, 46) and Friday comes from the Norse Goddess Freya, also known as Vanadis, whence **Vanadium** (V, 23).

Planets 4, Dwarf Planets 2 – **Mercury** (Hg, 80), Earth – **Tellerium** (Te, 52), Uranus – **Uranium** (U, 92), Neptune – **Neptunium** (Np, 93). The dwarf planets give us Pluto – **Plutonium** (Pu, 94), and Ceres – **Cerium** (Ce, 58).

THANK YOU

A beloved former panellist on *Round Britain Quiz* routinely used to lean back after a recording was over and sigh, 'The people who set these questions have *warped minds*.' The production team is indebted to a whole floating population of warped minds who have written for the show over the years. The work of Sue Barnard, David Edwards, Stephen Follows, Mark Mason, Stewart McCartney, Beth Porter and Danny Roth is excerpted here, with their generous permission. Listeners' ideas are also invaluable in the programmes, and some of the very cleverest of these are included in the final sections of the book.

RBQ might easily have died off in the mid-1990s, had Gaynor Vaughan Jones not entrusted this strange jewel of BBC radio heritage to one of her least experienced producers. My bosses have both provided support and allowed creative freedom ever since: Nicola Swords, Ian Bent and the late John Pidgeon, not to mention the successive Radio 4 controllers whose faith has ensured it's reached the age of 70 – and counting.

I've had the privilege of working with two brilliant presenters of *Round Britain Quiz*, Nick Clarke and Tom Sutcliffe, whose rock-solid and charming chairmanship has surely done more than anything to perpetuate the programme's success. Their wit and attention to detail are all over this book. There would also be no show without the panellists – too many since I took over to list, now, but all remarkable. Their erudition and epiphanies and agonies and exasperation guarantee weekly hilarity and drama. Lizzie Foster, Stephen Garner, Paul Hardy and Angela Sherwin have, successively and sometimes collaboratively, worked incredibly hard over the years to make sure the questions are factually accurate, and achieved many other cheerful organizational miracles to get *RBQ* on air.

Finally, a huge thank you to Nell Warner and her team for making a discursive cult radio show work so absorbingly on the printed page.

Paul Bajoria